Holy Helps for a Godly Life

SERIES EDITORS
Joel R. Beeke & Jay T. Collier

Interest in the Puritans continues to grow, but many people find the reading of these giants of the faith a bit unnerving. This series seeks to overcome that barrier by presenting Puritan books that are convenient in size and unintimidating in length. Each book is carefully edited with modern readers in mind, smoothing out difficult language of a bygone era while retaining the meaning of the original authors. Books for the series are thoughtfully selected to provide some of the best counsel on important subjects that people continue to wrestle with today.

Holy Helps for a Godly Life

Richard Rogers

Edited by
Brian G. Hedges

Reformation Heritage Books
Grand Rapids, Michigan

Holy Helps for a Godly Life
© 2018 by Reformation Heritage Books

Reformation Heritage Books
2965 Leonard St. NE
Grand Rapids, MI 49525
616-977-0889
orders@heritagebooks.org
www.heritagebooks.org

Printed in the United States of America
18 19 20 21 22 23/10 9 8 7 6 5 4 3 2 1

Library of Congress Cataloging-in-Publication Data

Names: Rogers, Richard, 1550?-1618, author. | Hedges, Brian G., editor.
Title: Holy helps for a godly life / Richard Rogers ; edited by Brian G.
    Hedges.
Description: Grand Rapids, Michigan : Reformation Heritage Books, 2018.
    | Series: Puritan treasures for today | Previously published as the third
    treatise of the Seaven treatises : London : Felix Kyngston for Thomas
    Man, 1610.
Identifiers: LCCN 2017061110 (print) | LCCN 2018005843 (ebook) |
    ISBN 9781601785978 (epub) | ISBN 9781601785961 (pbk. : alk. paper)
Subjects: LCSH: Christian life—Early works to 1800.
Classification: LCC BX9315 (ebook) | LCC BX9315 .R6 2018 (print) |
    DDC 248.4/6—dc23
LC record available at https://lccn.loc.gov/2017061110

For additional Reformed literature, request a free book list from Reformation Heritage Books at the above regular or e-mail address.

Table of Contents

Preface

Spiritual disciplines have now been a regular feature in evangelical teaching on discipleship for several decades. Interest in these disciplines surged following the 1978 publication of Richard Foster's *Celebration of Discipline*, such that dozens of similar titles now fill our shelves. This has been a good development to the degree that it has led believers into renewed habits of Bible reading, meditation, and prayer.

Many of these books, however, freely utilize the devotional writings of contemplatives and mystics from medieval Roman Catholicism, Jesuit writings from the Counter-Reformation, and the devotional writings of the Quakers. These are often quoted alongside Reformed, Puritan, and evangelical authors, while paying little attention to their original theological and ecclesiastical contexts.[1] The result is that much evangelical teaching

---

1. Several books are happy exceptions to this trend and mostly quote from devotional literature in the Puritan and Reformed

on devotional practices is only loosely connected to a robust understanding of the gospel of grace—or worse, it leads undiscerning believers into practices more characterized by mysticism, asceticism, and legalism than the gospel-grounded, grace-oriented piety of which Calvin spoke, "that reverence joined with love of God which the knowledge of his benefits induces."[2]

But godliness never flourishes unless it is planted in the fertile soil of God's grace. Legalism subverts the gospel and obscures the redemptive work of Christ on the cross, which removes the debt of sin and cancels the curse of the law (Gal. 1:6–9; 3:13–14; Col. 2:11–17). Mystical experience, unmoored from God's self-revelation in Scripture, leads to inflated emotionalism, but not genuine nourishment from Christ, the head of the body (Col. 2:18–19). And the practices of asceticism, while bearing a superficial resemblance to wisdom, are useless in truly mortifying the flesh (vv. 20–23).

The Puritans understood this and left behind for us the greatest library of biblical, evangelical (that is,

---

tradition. See especially Donald S. Whitney, *Spiritual Disciplines for the Christian Life* (Colorado Springs: NavPress, 2014); David Mathis, *Habits of Grace: Enjoying Jesus through Spiritual Disciplines* (Wheaton, Ill.: Crossway, 2016); and Murray G. Brett, *Growing Up in Grace: The Use of Means for Communion with God* (Grand Rapids: Reformation Heritage Books, 2009).

2. John Calvin, *Institutes of the Christian Religion*, ed. John T. McNeill, trans. Ford Lewis Battles (Philadelphia: Westminster Press, 1960), 1.2.1.

gospel-oriented), practical, devotional literature that the church has ever produced. At the headwaters of the Puritan movement, there was a "spiritual brotherhood" of pastors and preachers, centered in Cambridge, who were heirs of the preceding Reformers and fathers to the generations that followed.[3] This brotherhood included Lawrence Chaderton, William Perkins, Richard Greenham, John Downame, and Richard Rogers, the author of *Holy Helps for a Godly Life*. Together, these men became the leading "architects of the Puritan theology of godliness."[4]

Richard Rogers: "The Enoch of His Age"

Born in 1551, Richard Rogers was the son of a "joiner," or furniture maker. Thanks to the sponsorship of a wealthy patron, Rogers was educated at Christ's College, Cambridge, and graduated with a bachelor of arts in 1571. In 1574, he earned a master of arts from Caius College. The next year he became curate of Radminster in Essex and two years later was appointed lecturer at Wethersfield, Essex, where he would spend the next four decades of his life. Rogers was temporarily suspended

---

3. See Paul R. Schaefer Jr., *The Spiritual Brotherhood: Cambridge Puritans and the Nature of Christian Piety* (Grand Rapids: Reformation Heritage Books, 2011).

4. Joel Beeke and Randall J. Pederson, *Meet the Puritans: With a Guide to Modern Reprints* (Grand Rapids: Reformation Heritage Books, 2007), 188.

from his pulpit for nonconformity in 1583, and again in 1603. Though he had a reputation for austerity, his ministry was blessed with many conversions. Rogers's grandson William Jenkyn called him "the Enoch of his age," for Rogers walked with God and was sorry that each day was not his last.[5]

Rogers was not only a preacher and author—but also a husband and father. He had at least seven children with his first wife, Barbara. After her death, he married Susan Ward, the widow of another minister, becoming the stepfather to her six children. Of all these children, five—Daniel Rogers, Ezekiel Rogers, Samuel Ward, John Ward, and Nathaniel Ward—became Puritan ministers.

Rogers's diary reveals him to be a sincere and godly man who yet struggled with ongoing conflicts with sin and the flesh. He especially lamented four besetting sins that gave him most trouble: "'light thoughts' or 'roving fantasies'; 'liking of worldly profit' (financial gain, that is); 'unprofitableness' or ineffectiveness in communicating his attitude to others; and, lastly, neglect of study."[6] But his heart was bent toward God. As he wrote on

---

5. Beeke and Pederson, *Meet the Puritans*, 507. Unless otherwise noted, all bibliographical details in this preface are drawn from Beeke and Pederson's biographical sketch of Rogers in *Meet the Puritans*, 505–8.

6. M. M. Knappen, ed., *Two Elizabethan Puritan Diaries by Richard Rogers and Samuel Ward* (Chicago: American Society of Church History, 1933), 5. In this and all following excerpts from the diary, I have updated spelling and grammar to reflect modern use.

November 17, 1587, "I have firmly purposed to make my whole life a meditation of a better life, and godliness in every part even mine occupation and trade, that I may from point to point and from step to step with more watchfulness walk with the Lord. Oh the infinite gain of it."[7] And on November 29, 1587, "And this is mine hearty desire that I may make godliness, I mean one part or other of it, to be my delight through my whole life."[8]

Seven Treatises: A Christian Travel Guide

Though not as famous as William Perkins (not to mention John Owen, Richard Baxter, and other pastor-theologians of subsequent generations), Rogers was a significant leader among nonconformists in Elizabethan England. Rogers, like Enoch, walked with God. And he wrote a massive travel guide to help fellow pilgrims in their journey.

This guide, Rogers's most important contribu-tion to Puritan literature, was called *Seven Treatises*. One scholarly source names Rogers as one of "the most influential of the spiritual authors," noting that *Seven Treatises* "went through six editions between 1603 and 1630, with a further five editions of an abridgment by Stephen Egerton.... The influence of [*Seven Treatises*] can be traced in the lives of a whole generation of Puritan

---

7. Knappen, *Two Elizabethan Puritan Diaries*, 64.
8. Knappen, *Two Elizabethan Puritan Diaries*, 65.

Preface

laymen."[9] In the words of William Haller, "*Seven Treatises* was the first important exposition of the code of behavior which expressed the English Calvinist, or more broadly speaking, the Puritan conception of the spiritual and moral life. As such it inaugurated a literature the extent and influence of which in all departments of life can hardly be exaggerated."[10] It will be helpful for us to consider the purpose, scope, and importance of this book.

Purpose

The full title of the book reveals its purpose:

SEVEN TREATISES
CONTAINING SUCH DIRECTION
AS IS GATHERED OUT OF THE
HOLY SCRIPTURES,
LEADING AND GUIDING
to true happiness, both in this life, and
in the life to come:
and may be called the practice
of *Christianity*.

---

9. Patrick Collinson, Arnold Hunt, and Alexandra Walsam, "Religious Publishing in England 1557–1640," in *The Cambridge History of the Book in Britain, Volume IV, 1557–1695*, ed. John Barnard, D. F. McKenzie, and Maureen Bell (Cambridge: Cambridge University Press, 2002), 42.

10. William Haller, *The Rise of Puritanism* (New York: Columbia University Press, 1938), 36. Quoted in Beeke and Pederson, *Meet the Puritans*, 506.

PROFITABLE FOR ALL SUCH AS
HEARTILY DESIRE THE SAME:
IN THE WHICH,

more particularly true Christians may learn how to lead
a godly and comfortable life every day,
notwithstanding their tribulations.[11]

This book, then, was practical in its focus, a manual
or guidebook that marked out the scriptural signposts
for walking in the way of the Lord, as it directed the
earnest Christian in the pursuit of true happiness, the
practice of godliness, and the path to eternal life. It was,
in fact, written as a distinctively *Protestant* guidebook
to counteract and correct the popular Roman Catholic
devotional manuals of the Jesuits and their tendency
to "ensnare and entangle the minds of ignorant and
simple Christians, in the corrupt and filthy puddle of
Popish devotion."[12]

Scope

The scope of the *Seven Treatises* is remarkably comprehensive, as indicated by the following descriptions of
each treatise (each of which contains between ten and
twenty chapters):

---

11. Richard Rogers, *Seven Treatises* (London: Felix Kynston, for
Thomas Man, 1616), title page. In this and all subsequent references,
I have updated the spelling and grammar to reflect modern use.

12. "To the Christian Reader," in Rogers, *Seven Treatises.*

The first treatise shows who are the true children of God.

The second treatise declares at large, what the life of the true believer is, and the conversation [behavior] of such as have assured hope of salvation.

The third treatise lays forth the means, whereby a godly life is helped and continued.

The fourth treatise directs the believer unto a daily practice of a Christian life.

The fifth treatise shows the lets [hindrances] which hinder the sincere course of the Christian life before described.

The sixth treatise sets down the privileges which belong to every true Christian: and how he may have his part in them.

The seventh treatise contains the objections and cavils [complaints], which may be brought against the doctrine before set down, and answer[s] to them.[13]

The whole project, therefore, covered everything from the nature of true conversion (treatise 1), its moral, ethical outworking in a life of godliness (treatise 2), and

---

13. "The Sum of All the Seven Treatises, and the Contents of Every Chapter in Them," in Rogers, *Seven Treatises*.

the means for nourishing and maintaining such a life (treatise 3), to the daily practice of Christianity (treatise 4), the manifold hindrances that confront the Christian walking this path (treatise 5), the privileges that sustain his hope along the way (treatise 6), and a final wrap-up treatise answering objections to all that came before (treatise 7).

A basic understanding of this superstructure will be important for knowing how best to read and profit from the present volume, which is a modernized abridgment of treatise 3.

Importance

We should also note the importance of the *Seven Treatises*, especially treatise 3. As O. R. Johnston observed, "Rogers' work is of paramount importance here, for he seems to have been the first man explicitly to state the nature and aims of Meditation as a Scriptural means of grace."[14] In fact, Rogers was the first Puritan to treat these means in a systematic and cohesive way. Though Luther, Calvin, and other Reformers had written much about prayer and the sacraments, and though general exhortations to devotional practices were scattered in the sermons and treatises of Perkins and Greenham, Rogers was apparently the first Protestant to compile a

---

14. O. R. Johnston, "The Means of Grace in Puritan Theology," *The Evangelical Quarterly* 25, no. 4 (1953): 212.

full list of the means of grace, both public and private, to help Christians in the pursuit of godliness.[15]

Rogers was also a pioneer in explaining the pieces of the Christian armor from Ephesians 6 for the believer's devotional benefit and growth in godliness. Readers who are already familiar with Puritan literature will know of William Gurnall's *The Christian in Complete Armour*, which was published in three parts in 1655, 1658, and 1662.[16] Less well-known is John Downame's *The Christian Warfare*, its four parts having been published separately from 1609 to 1618.[17] But Rogers predates both.

The importance of Rogers's work is also seen in its thoroughness. As fellow minister Ezekiel Culverwel said

---

15. Although one might say this honor belongs to Richard Greenham's *Godly Instruction for the Due Examination and Direction of All Good Men for the Attaining and Retaining of Faith and a Good Conscience*. Published posthumously by Henry Holland in 1599, this treatise contains seventy-five alphabetically arranged chapters on a myriad of subjects, ranging from admonition to zeal. Greenham includes numerous means to godliness, such as baptism (ch. 8), keeping watch over our hearts (chs. 34–35), hearing God's word (ch. 36), prayer and meditation (ch. 58), and the sacraments (ch. 61). Other chapters address both doctrinal topics (like justification, regeneration, and sanctification) and practical moral issues (like anger, matrimony, and temptation). Rogers's *Seven Treatises*, published a few years later, marks an advance in both the scope and organization of Protestant devotional material.

16. Beeke and Pederson, *Meet the Puritans*, 306.

17. Beeke and Pederson, *Meet the Puritans*, 188.

in a preface to the *Seven Treatises*: "In my simple opinion it might in one principal respect be called the Anatomy of the soul, wherein not only the great and principal parts are laid open, but every vein and little nerve are so discovered, that we may as it were, with the eye behold, as the right constitution of the whole and every part of a true Christian; so the manifold defects and imperfections thereof."[18]

Holy Helps for a Godly Life

As mentioned above, the present volume, *Holy Helps for a Godly Life*, is an abridged modernization of Rogers's third treatise, which "lays forth the means, whereby a godly life is helped and continued." These means or helps (the terms are interchangeable for Rogers) are the spiritual disciplines, or what believers in the Reformed tradition sometimes call the "means of grace." Though Rogers himself does not use the term "means of grace," it may be helpful to define this phrase, which can be used in both a narrower and broader sense.

In the narrower sense, the means of grace refer to the ordinary channels through which God communicates His grace to men—namely, the preaching of the word, the sacraments, and prayer.[19] These means do not

---

18. "To the Christian Reader," in Rogers, *Seven Treatises*.

19. As Charles Hodge writes, "By means of grace are not meant every instrumentality which God may please to make the means of spiritual edification to his children. The phrase is intended to

work *ex opere operato*—that is, in a magical or mechanical way, conferring grace in and of themselves, so that any recipient of the external sacraments thereby also necessarily and automatically receives grace. The means are rather channels through which God communicates His grace to the believer, who receives this grace through the divine gift of faith.

In the broader sense, the means of grace are synonymous with spiritual disciplines, including such practices as Bible reading, meditation, private prayer, and fasting. In Puritan and later evangelical devotional literature, this latter, broader understanding is common.[20]

While Rogers does not use the full phrase "means of grace," he does use the term "means" often, calling the focus of his third treatise, "the means whereby a godly life is helped and continued." In his introductory remarks, Rogers explains, "The Christian life is upheld and continued by means. Everyone who sets upon this life will desire to know these means and how to rightly use them, because the hindrances and discouragements

---

indicate those institutions which God has ordained to be the ordinary channels of grace, *i.e.*, of the supernatural influences of the Holy Spirit, to the souls of men. The means of grace, according to the standards of our Church, are the word, sacraments, and prayer." *Systematic Theology* (Oak Harbor, Wash.: Logos Research Systems, 1997), 3:466.

20. For example, see Walter Marshall, *The Gospel Mystery of Sanctification* (Grand Rapids: Reformation Heritage Books, 1999), direction 13.

in the Christian life are many and great. It is therefore fitting for me to show what I understand by these means or helps.... As the Christian life does not begin without means, neither can it grow without them." In defining these means or helps, Rogers says, "The means God has appointed to help His people to continue and grow in a godly life, are those religious exercises, by which Christians may be made fit to practice it." These he divides into ordinary and extraordinary and public and private.

The public (and ordinary) means are the preaching of the word, the sacraments, and public prayers, with the singing of psalms. Rogers lists seven private (also ordinary) helps—namely, watchfulness, meditation, putting and keeping on the Christian armor, reflection on personal spiritual experience, godly conversation with other believers and within one's family, private prayer, and the reading of both Scripture and godly literature. Finally, Rogers addresses two extraordinary means: solemn thanksgiving and fasting.

Some of these helps, such as watchfulness or the Christian armor, are surprising. These are rarely, if ever, included in contemporary books on spiritual disciplines. Rogers's treatment of other helps, especially godly conversation ("the use of company"), is disappointingly brief. This is because he addressed it elsewhere in the overall project of *Seven Treatises*. In other cases, Rogers is brief because the help in question was more familiar to the original audience.

Readers will benefit from Rogers most when they keep two things in mind. First, these helps are for Christians—that is, for true believers who have rested in the finished work of Christ for their justification. This is assumed by Rogers throughout, since he had already established it in the first treatise where he treats both man's misery (ch. 2) and God's way of redemption from it (ch. 3)—that is, the way of faith alone in Christ alone. Rogers could hardly be clearer on this point. "There is no way to receive Christ and all His merits (the full medicine of man's misery) but by faith," he writes. And what is faith? Rogers continues:

> Now this true faith (which for the worthy effect of it, we call justifying faith,) is nothing else but a sound belief in that promise of life, that poor sinners coming unto Christ, He will ease them (Matt. 11:28), that is, free them from all woe, and restore them to all happiness here and forever (Acts 26:18; Heb. 4:1); and to be short, so to give credit to God's Word (Rom. 10:17), as they rest thereon that He will save them.
>
> This true faith is wrought in them by the ministry of the Word, revealing this mercy and truth of God. And by these, the Holy Ghost enlightening them to conceive, and drawing them to believe, and so uniting them to Christ. Whoever receives this, is hereby made the child

of God (so as he himself will see it) and an inheritor by sure hope of eternal life.

This therefore is to be known of him who will be saved, and his judgment is to be settled in this truth, before he enjoys it as his own, or can have his part in it. He must be able to see clearly and soundly, that God has made this Christ Jesus His Son Lord over all creatures (Acts 2:36), Conqueror of the devils, Deliverer of the captives, and Comforter of the heavy hearts: so that by Him there is as full pardon of sin purchased (Rom. 5:15), as ever was by Adam procured guiltiness and condemnation.[21]

Second, the aim of these helps is to lead believers into both holiness and happiness. Remember the overall purpose of the *Seven Treatises* as expressed in the title: "leading and guiding to true happiness, both in this life, and in the life to come...in the which...true Christians may learn how to lead a godly and comfortable life every day, notwithstanding their tribulations." Rogers knew what modern believers sometimes forget: holiness is the way to true happiness. Discipline, though a restriction of sorts, leads to greater freedom. Godliness is the indispensable key to a comfortable life (that is, a life filled with spiritual comforts).

---

21. Rogers, *Seven Treatises*, 9.

Rogers does not leave his readers wondering what he meant by godliness, for this is the subject of the second treatise, which "declares at large, what the life of the true believer is, and the conversation [behavior] of such as have assured hope of salvation." In the exposition that follows, Rogers delineates the necessary ingredients to a godly life: unfeigned faith; faith in the temporal promises of God and hearty assent to the commands and threats in Scripture; a cleansed heart; the renunciation of all sins, both inward and outward; the virtues of uprightness, diligence, continuance, humility, and meekness; and the fulfillment of our duties to both God and man, as expounded through the Ten Commandments.[22]

There is nothing innovative in this approach. Readers can easily glean the same teaching from books 2 and 3 in Calvin's *Institutes* or from later Puritan authors, such as Thomas Watson. The real value of Rogers here is his thoroughness and precision. In an often-repeated story, Rogers was once riding with the lord of a nearby manor, who said, "Mr. Rogers, I like you and your company very well, only you are too precise." Rogers replied, "Oh, sir, I serve a very precise God." This precision in godliness is the goal for which we discipline ourselves. As Paul told Timothy, "Exercise thyself rather unto godliness. For bodily exercise profiteth little: but godliness is profitable

---

22. Rogers, *Seven Treatises*, 9. See also "The Sum of All the Seven Treatises, and the Contents of Every Chapter in Them," in the front matter of Rogers, *Seven Treatises*.

unto all things, having promise of the life that now is, and of that which is to come" (1 Tim. 4:7b–8). Spiritual disciplines, or helps, are the means to this end.

A Note on the Editing

This book is both a modernization and an abridgement of Rogers's third treatise. Archaic words have been replaced with modern words. Long, complex sentences have been broken down into shorter, simpler sentences. When appropriate, marginal notes have been revised and inserted into the text as headings. In other places, I have added headings. Many redundancies and irrelevant asides have been removed, while other material has been condensed. The appendix, "Helps for Meditation," was originally in a chapter on rules and examples of meditation. I have included it as an appendix because it serves as a convenient summary of Rogers's teaching in this treatise. Other material from that chapter has either been combined with chapter 6 (on meditation) or has been removed. These changes were deemed best for bringing Rogers's work into the twenty-first century, but I have sought to preserve the substance of Rogers's teaching without adding anything to his content.

In John Bunyan's *Pilgrim's Progress*, there is a scene when Christian comes to the Interpreter's House and is brought into a candlelit room. Bunyan writes, "Christian saw the picture of a very grave person against the wall; and this was the fashion of it. It had eyes lifted up to Heaven, the best of books in his hand, the law of truth was written upon his lips, the world was behind his back. It stood as if it pleaded with men, and a crown of gold did hang over its head." When Christian asks what this means, his guide explains that this man is "one of a thousand; he can beget children (1 Cor. 4:15), travail in birth with children (Gal. 4:19), and nurse them himself when they are born." The grave man's work is to "know and unfold dark things to sinners." And for love of his Master, he has turned his back on this present world and awaits his reward in the glorious world to come. The Interpreter further explains that it is only such a man "whom the Lord of the place whither thou art going, hath authorized to be thy guide in all difficult places thou mayest meet with in the way."[23]

Richard Rogers was such a man. He will prove a worthy guide on your own pilgrimage to the Celestial City.

—Brian G. Hedges
August 2017

---

23. John Bunyan, *The Pilgrim's Progress* (Carlisle, Pa.: Banner of Truth, 1977), 25–26.

INTRODUCTION

Means to Living a Godly Life

Believers must walk in a safe and godly way throughout their pilgrimage to heaven. But the Christian life is upheld and continued by means.

Everyone who sets upon this life will desire to know these means and how to rightly use them, because the hindrances and discouragements in the Christian life are many and great. It is therefore fitting for me to show what I understand by these means or helps. What are they, what is their nature, and how should they be used? God has promised to give grace to those who use these means in a right and reverent way in order to enable them to live a godly life. As the Christian life does not begin without means, neither can it grow without them.

The goodness and kindness of our God is seen in His ordaining these means for our great benefit and comfort. In the same way, it is necessary for us to use them with the degree of care and constancy as will make them most profitable to us. Only in this way will we discover in these means the fruit that God has promised.

What Are the Means God Appointed?

The means God has appointed to help His people continue and grow in a godly life are those religious exercises by which Christians may be made fit to practice godliness. These means include both the ordinary and the extraordinary. The ordinary means are those which should be regularly used, while the extraordinary are those which are only used occasionally for a special time, such as fasting, or for rare solemnities in feasting and thanksgiving. Both sorts of means (ordinary and extraordinary) are either public or private.

Public Means
The public means, which are ordinarily used in our public assemblies, are these three.

1. The ministry of the word read, preached, and heard, as the Lord prescribes

2. The administration and worthy receiving of the holy sacraments

3. The exercise of prayer with thanksgiving and singing of psalms

Private Means
But we cannot daily use and enjoy the public means (though we need daily relief and help); and even if we

could, the public means are not sufficient to enable us to honor God as we should or as He commands us. Therefore, God has commanded us to use private exercises, especially the following seven:

1. Watchfulness
2. Meditation
3. The armor of a Christian
4. Reflecting on our own experience
5. The use of company by godly conversation[1] and family exercises
6. Prayer
7. Reading

The first four belong to each individual believer; the fifth believers use with others; and the last two can be used by both individuals *and* in company with others.

The necessity of these private helps is so great that if they are not known and rightly used, the public means will prove unprofitable, and, as we will see in future chapters, the believer's Christian life will lose its proper shape.

This briefly explains what the means for living a godly life are and what specific practices they include.

---

1. Rogers's original term is "conference," often used by the Puritans to refer to the practice of intentional godly conversation with fellow believers. For more, see Joanne J. Jung, *Godly Conversations: Rediscovering the Puritan Practice of Conference* (Grand Rapids: Reformation Heritage Books, 2011).

In future chapters, I will more fully explain the nature and use of each one of these means, and how God works through them to uphold the weight of a godly life. In this way, all who desire to wisely consider these means may do so. And those who use these means will discover their value for themselves. First, I will begin with the public means and afterward speak of the private.

And I will so handle and speak of each one according to the skill which God has given me, as may make most for this present purpose: I will more fully explain those means which are lesser known and more briefly treated than those with which men are most acquainted.

Though the Means Are Duties, They Are Also Helps

For those who object that I have called these means "helps," whereas the same means are elsewhere described as parts of our Christian duty, I do not deny that they are duties. But though they are duties, they are also helps. In fact, the duties we will consider here (such as hearing the word, receiving the sacraments, watching, prayer, and the others) are rightly called "helps" because they fit us for the right performance of all other duties.

CHAPTER 1

The Ministry of the Word

We begin therefore with the public means and helps, which God has appointed to strengthen the believer and settle him in a godly life. The ministry of the word is the first and principal of these means.

The Attributes of the Scriptures

This comes as no surprise when we consider the royal and most excellent commendations that we hear and read concerning the canonical Scriptures, which are this word of God.

Excellency and Power

The Scriptures are proved by good evidence and testimony to be the very truth of the word of God (and not the fantasies of men). This is seen in both the excellency of the matter contained in the Scriptures (Ps. 119:129) and by the mighty operation of the Scriptures (Heb. 4:12). God commands us to search these Scriptures

(John 5:39) and sends us to them if we desire to know His mind and will toward us.

Authority

The authority of the Scriptures is such that we do not need to be troubled by those who oppose them or call them into question. For even if it were an angel from heaven (Gal. 1:8) (if this were possible), much less the Man of Sin, who yet challenges authority to be heard before the Scriptures, we should not be troubled.

Sufficiency

We are also taught that the Scriptures are all-sufficient, so that we may not doubt that all God's will is revealed in them (2 Tim. 3:16). The Scriptures thus contain those things necessary to make us true Christians and the inheritors of salvation, in which our true happiness consists.

Clarity

The plainness of the heavenly matter contained in the Scriptures by the means which God has used and the order that He has taken for laying out their sweetness and beauty (Matt. 11:25) is evident in that the most necessary points are easy to be understood even by the simple and ignorant (Prov. 14:6).

The Gifts of Pastors and Teachers

In addition to this, God has commanded the Scriptures to be reverently and distinctly read in the assembly and has given unto His church the most excellent gifts of pastors and teachers (Eph. 4:11). God has given pastors and teachers to interpret and teach His whole counsel out of the Scriptures and to show His people how to profit by its teaching and to make the right use thereof by applying the Scriptures to His people, as if they had been particularly and only appointed for them.

In like manner, God has provided to have the Holy Scriptures translated into the various languages of the world, so that they, like the good people of Thessalonica and Berea, might compare the sermons heard in their own tongue with the Scriptures and so find more clear light and comfort by them (Acts 17:11).

Considering all this, it is not hard to see what a singular help the sound, ordinary ministry of the word is in building up the weak Christian into a stronger, more godly life. For God has appointed this preaching of His word to perfect the faith of His elect (1 Thess. 3:10). That is why Peter charges the shepherds to feed the flock of Christ, which depends upon them (1 Peter 5:2), just as our Savior (Peter's teacher) required Peter to demonstrate his love for Him by feeding His lambs and His sheep (John 21:15). When the word is preached with authority and power to persuade, not as the weak and frothy word of man, but as it is indeed, the word

of the living God (1 Thess. 2:13), it is mighty in operation and sharper than any two-edged sword (Heb. 4:12),
working God's people as a strong medicine upon a disease. And thus the ministry of the word becomes the
power of God unto salvation to them.

Benefits from the Ministry of the Word

Let us now consider the many uses and daily helps that
God's people have through the ministry of the word.
This is to say nothing of the benefit of this ordinance
to the unregenerate, who yet still walk in darkness. For
though the ministry of the word is a mighty and great
means to convert the unregenerate from their old way of
life and from the power and bondage of Satan unto God
(Acts 26:18; 1 Cor. 14:24), our main purpose here is to
behold the benefit of this means to the regenerate.

Knowledge
First, by the ministry of the word God's people are
cleared from error and darkness concerning both piety
and behavior, and they grow more sound in the knowledge of the truth. Without this ministry, they are fraught
and encumbered with error. But by use of this means
they come to see more particularly into the way and
whole course of Christianity. When God's children lack
this, they are unsettled and held in ignorance and blindness concerning many needful points. Thus they bear
less fruit in the Christian life and become dim patterns
of holiness to others. Furthermore, those who use these

means diligently and reverently grow daily settled and established in their knowledge (2 Peter 1:12; 3:17). But those who are destitute of this gracious help will lack this (although they may have some benefit by private reading).

Renewal

Again, this means quickens them in their drowsiness, cheers them in their heaviness, and calls them back from their wanderings. It raises them up when they have fallen and counsels them in their doubtful cases. And through their experience of God's dealing with them in all situations, this preaching of the word of God is ordinarily a means through which they are firmly settled in a godly course. It helps them to keep well when they are well, rather than grow fickle and inconstant in the carrying of themselves well, as many are. This renewal is a great benefit, sought by many with tears, yet obtained only by few.

Sanctification

Even those who have weak beginnings in the church can attain and grow through the ministry of the word. For when God's will is laid forth in preaching in a sound, plain, and orderly manner, many people are helped so to "gird up the loins of their minds." They thus learn to lay aside and cast off that which would hinder them, especially their inward corruptions. And they prepare themselves to follow the directions which lead and guide them to their duty. By this they discover their weaknesses and how they are held back when they have fallen. By this they learn the right way of moving forward. The more frequently people are thus put in mind of these things, the better. In other words, the ministry of the word is the sun which gives light to them in all places and the rule by which they frame all their actions. Even a weak Christian, therefore, when he desires to learn, will in this way grow in living a godly life.

Private Reading

In addition to all I have said, the true Christian by his ordinary hearing is taught to give some of his time to reading the Scriptures (and other good writers, as is said in another place[1]), and this with good fruit, understanding, and comfort. Without the public ministry of the word, the Christian is likely to neglect and become weary of the labor of private reading and instead give himself to idleness or vain activities. Even if he should use the private means, without the public ministry of the word he will do so with less knowledge, comfort, or any other profit.

Example to Others

When a person is thus framed by the ministry of the word, he becomes a light and example to others, having found such great help by this means himself. Therefore:

---

1. See chapter 11, "Reading," for Rogers's specific recommendations.

- if he may ordinarily by the preaching of the word "be led into all truth" necessary for him to know and be delivered from error in religion and manners;

- if he may "be established and confirmed in the knowledge of the will of God";

- if he may be daily reformed in his affections and life, more and more increasing therein and overcoming himself better thereby;

- if he may both be brought to give time (as his calling will permit) in reading and find profit thereby;

- and finally, if he may "in time become an example" of a godly life unto others,

then I may boldly affirm and conclude that the ordinary preaching of the word is a singular means whereby God has provided that His people should grow and increase in a godly life.

Hindrances to Benefiting from the Ministry of the Word

If what I have said is granted, I say no more but this: I would to God that those who are greatly esteemed for their religion and often hear the word were helped in all these ways unto godliness. But, God knows, it is seldom so. When this sound and plain teaching is lacking, therefore, how much more will the people be out of frame?

But where the minister cannot be faulted with lack of diligence, skill, love, and plainness in a good order of teaching, it is certain that the fault is in the hearers. Though they otherwise may belong to the Lord, yet they are either not reverent and attentive in hearing, are not prepared before to hear, or else do not digest willingly that which they have heard. They are instead filled with dangerous qualities in their lives or corruptions in their hearts. Among these corruptions, one especially hinders them: when they esteem the doctrine of the word no greater than they esteem the one who teaches.

Now if in this one means such great help may be received, what may be thought when this and others work together?

An Exhortation

I conclude with this exhortation: Feed the Lord's flock which depends upon you, and be instant in season, and out of season, O ministers of the Lord. Know the day of your visitation, and the things which belong to your peace (1 Peter 5:2; 2 Tim. 4:2; Luke 19:44) by preaching, O people, who live under the ministry of the word. Lay up now in your harvest against the time of your necessity, and be persuaded that you need all that you gather. Seek to enjoy this liberty of the ministry of the word, you that lack it. And if you may enjoy it as easily and with as little pain as you do your market, think it worth your labor. Buy wisdom whatever it costs you, but "sell it not" (Prov. 23:23), whatever you may get for it. Pray the Lord of the harvest to thrust forth laborers plentifully into the harvest (Matt. 9:38), you that are "white already to harvest" (John 4:35) to be labored among and desirous to be brought into the Lord's barn, among whom faithful and diligent laborers are lacking.

Lastly, to all you that have the oversight of the Lord's ministry, see that those who are called to the ministry teach soundly, plainly, faithfully, and diligently. And go before them yourselves painstakingly, "as lights and good examples," that "many thanks may be given, and prayers made to God by the people for you," when you will give them so good occasion to remember you. And in that day of accounts, may you have many to witness the godly care you had over them, and how you warmed their hearts and comforted them with such good diet for their souls and liberal provision from the Word.

We have thus considered the first public help for the increasing and nourishing of a godly and Christian life in all such as have truly entered the Christian life—namely, the public help of the word preached.

CHAPTER 2

The Sacraments

The second public help or means is the sacraments. Of the two, the sacraments are less understood than the ministry of the word and so are considered less helpful to godliness. This is because Christians have less frequent use of the sacraments than the ministry of the word, and because they are not as fully instructed regarding their use. Of the two sacraments which God has left to His church in this latter age to be enjoyed, baptism is less seen and perceived to be a help than the Lord's Supper. In speaking of this, my only purpose is to show the Christian reader how the sacraments are means and helps to set him forward in a godly life and to leave other knowledge about the sacraments to ordinary teaching and to those who have written of them at large, such as Peter Martyr Vermigli, John Calvin, and Theodore Beza.[1]

---

1. See chapter 11, "Reading," for Rogers's recommendations of specific books from these authors.

The Sacraments Confirm the Teaching of the Word

This also I will do with as much brevity as I can. Therefore, seeing first that the sacraments are helps necessarily joined to the preaching of the word, and that they visibly confirm and ratify the teaching of the word, and that by the sacraments the covenant made between God and the believer is most surely sealed, by this it appears how the sacraments are helps both to the strengthening of faith and giving encouragement to living a godly life.

To make this clearer, let it be understood that God has freely granted to all the faithful that He will never call their sins to a reckoning, but will be their God and love them to the end through Christ (John 13:1). And to confirm this promise, He has sealed it in the sacrament by so evident and infallible a sign as cannot deceive. The sacrament, therefore, always remains to faithful receivers as a clear witness that the benefits God has promised are theirs. As often as any doubts arise in their hearts through weakness, they are hereby removed. That is why the apostle Paul calls them a "seal of the righteousness of the faith" (Rom. 4:11).

What God and Believers Covenant to One Another in the Sacraments

As God has covenanted for His part, so every believer has covenanted in his own behalf to always trust in God and to endeavor to walk before Him continually in uprightness of heart and innocency of hands.

The sacrament is a sign of his sincerity by which having received he has openly professed the consecration of himself to the Lord, that he is now no more his own to live according to the desires of the flesh (Rom. 12:1; 1 Peter 4:1–2). Therefore, though the sacrament is not always being received, is it not always before his eyes, as it were, to tell him, what God has done? Yes, and that not rashly nor by constraint, but with good advice, as knowing that He will never have cause to repent of so doing, seeing that the Christian believes and that strength will be given to him by God to perform that which He has promised and sealed.

Is not then the sacrament a continual help, urging the believer to keep his covenant? Is he not by the fresh remembrance of it encouraged against temptations, weariness of doing his duty, and other such hindrances? Does it not cause him to say against them all, "How can I that am dead to sin, live any longer in it?" (Rom. 6:2)? To others, the sacrament is a "mystery, and hidden thing." As a book written in Hebrew or Greek, which an uneducated man finds unprofitable and says "I cannot read it," even though the book contains fruitful information if a skillful reader takes it in hand—in like manner, though those ignorant of truth find no help nor benefit by the sacraments, yet the true believer, having been soundly instructed, beholds much in them to encourage and set him forward in the godly life, having confidence in God's favor. He is also helped by the sacraments because God, who cannot lie, is to be believed.

For the edifying of the simple, this may be seen particularly in the two sacraments of our church—namely, baptism and the Lord's Supper.

How Baptism Is a Means

Every faithful Christian who has been baptized may have this benefit from baptism as long as he lives: that as by his engrafting into Christ he is one with Him and therefore sees that while Christ lives he must and will live also, so thus having perpetual union and fellowship with Christ, the believer draws strength and grace from Him, even as the branch draws strength from the vine, so that he may live the Christian life. If Christ then has the power of renewing him—which is signified and sealed by baptism (namely, the power of Christ's death mortifying sin and the virtue of His resurrection in raising him up to a new life)—is not baptism throughout his life, as often as he seriously considers it, a powerful means to help him forward in a Christian life?

How the Lord's Supper Is a Means

So, in the Lord's Supper, the faithful communicant in frequently receiving it is not only assured by the bread and wine that his soul may be comforted by Christ, but is also spiritually strengthened to all good duties. The believer thus finds a most sovereign help by the Lord's Supper to grow up unto a perfect age in Christ Jesus.

And this will more appear when we consider how many ways the faithful Christian is furthered in ordering and amending his life thereby, in (1) preparing himself for the Lord's Supper before he comes; (2) in the actual partaking of the Lord's Supper when he comes; and (3) after enjoying the Lord's Supper. These three aspects may serve as well as a perpetual rule for the faithful by which to examine themselves to always direct them in the right use of this sacrament and to prove that the sacraments are great helps to godliness.

Preparing to Receive the Lord's Supper

This is the way believers should prepare themselves to receive the Lord's Supper with profit:

First, that each believer test himself in these things: whether he has the knowledge of man's misery, redemption, and renewing, and of the resurrection and eternal life, and of the nature and benefit of that sacrament, along with the knowledge of other principal points—all which it is fitting that he should have if he would draw comfort from it.

Secondly, let him hold fast to his faith in the promises of salvation which God has wrought in him before by the preaching of the gospel. Such faith must not be lacking but held firmly or recovered after particular falls.

Thirdly, he must keep his heart diligently (Prov. 4:23) by renouncing and subduing all sin and being ready for any duty to which he is called.

Fourthly, and more particularly, let the believer have nothing in his heart against any man or woman, not even if they are his utter enemies. But let him "be reconciled" to them (Matt. 5:24) and be at peace with them, as he desires to be with the Lord.

And, fifthly, the believer being thus qualified should desire (as he has opportunity) to be a partaker of this sacrament and to receive the benefit God offers by it. And this is the way believers should examine themselves to determine if they are welcome guests to the Lord's Table.

However, much sloth, forgetfulness, darkness, corruption, and weakness quickly grows up even in good men, thus choking these previously mentioned gifts of God to the degree that even though such believers have at times found all these qualities in themselves, yet when the time for receiving the Lord's Supper comes, they cannot find them. God therefore gives this special charge, that if any of His people upon coming to the Lord's Supper find that these graces have by their own negligence become weakened, dimmed, and decayed, then they should not rashly come to the Table, but should speedily seek to recover themselves again. This they will do by a due examination of their situation according to the previously mentioned rules.

Those who find this difficult and find that they are not prepared as they have been in the past should be humbled. The fault is their own for neglecting to keep themselves in spiritual health. Therefore, let them not cease until they recover.

And this is how they are to recover themselves. Let them go apart by themselves and lay all other things aside to seriously consider what troubles their conscience. Let nothing be omitted. Then, whatever is found amiss (whether sloth, carelessness, worldliness, distrust, uncharitableness, or any other sin), let it be heartily mourned, acknowledged, and renounced (Prov. 28:13). Finally, let them recover their faith by laying hold of God's mercy and recover repentance by renewing their covenant with God. This is how those who have fallen should prepare themselves to receive the Lord's Supper. Such preparation is one of the three things required for those who would profit from this help.

Can this preparation be anything less than a great help to all who would enjoy it? Consider the person who was before snared in the world, who had been filled with strong corruption, as with poison, who had fallen into some particular sins and had neglected the nourishing of his faith, or had been at some bitter variance with his neighbor (or had done any such other like thing). Now, by this preparation, he repents and returns. Does he not by this find a singular help to the recovering of his strength?

Now consider the person who has committed none of these offenses and therefore does not need to offer such violence to himself, but has kept a Christian course and followed a good direction to the peace of his conscience. Yet as often as he comes to the Sacrament, preparing himself for it, will he not be confirmed, established, and settled more strongly in his Christian duties when he finds through self-examination that he is a suitable and welcome guest at the Lord's Table? Will this not comfort him at many other times, as often as he remembers that he has received the Lord's Table and may do so again?

We see, then, that even the preparation for the Lord's Supper is a great means to godliness.

While Receiving the Lord's Supper
Now to come to the action itself, when a man rightly prepared enjoys the present benefit of the Sacrament and is comforted there and made glad by the words of Christ Himself, the maker of the banquet, who bids him welcome and to be joyful, saying His body, "which is meat indeed" (John 6:55), and His blood (which is the only wholesome and savory drink) are prepared for him—how can he not be much encouraged and given progress in a Christian course, when he is thus revived and quickened in his soul with the spiritual food which he feeds upon by true faith, no less sensibly than he eats the bread and drinks the wine?

And yet I will say this: if this rejoicing at the Lord's hospitality were either hollow on behalf of Him that bids (as it is with many men who invite others to their table), or only a temporary and earthly benefit on behalf of the receiver, then it would not be accounted so highly. But it is far otherwise—namely, it is a benefit without comparison both in goodness and permanence. It is a continual feast. Therefore, it has great power to stir up observers to honor God. For this reason, the communicant, admiring the goodness and kindness of God declared to him in the Sacrament, breaks forth into praise and says, "O LORD, Thou hast made me drunk with the wine of Thy cellar! How sweet is Thy love, and Thy kindness past finding out? What will I render to the LORD for all His mercies?" (see Song 2:4; Ps. 116:12).

Is it now difficult to discern how this heavenly banquet, in the reception of it, enlarges the heart of the faithful servant of God and makes him fit for duty and fills his heart with comfort, while he communes in the Supper with the rest of the faithful, so welcome to the Lord, who invited him to it? For at the Supper he can and should meditate on the blessing of the banquet, on the love of Him who ordained it, on the communion he has with Christ, on His graces, on the outward signs and what they assure him of, and on the word preached, which shows him all these things. For although the flesh strives against the Spirit (Gal. 5:17) as well in this as in other works and actions, yet the faithful communicant in his measure finds his heart ready to yield up to the Lord in this heavenly banquet the sacrifice of praise and thanks, though all do it not in a like measure.

After Receiving the Lord's Supper

We now come to the third point, which carries the same force. After a believer has received the Sacrament and enjoyed the benefit bestowed upon him in it to encourage him onward and strengthen him to every good work, the Sacrament is a help. Just as a person is refreshed by eating a meal and is strengthened for labor, so also, when rightly used according to God's appointment through remembrance and due consideration of God's kindness offered and received in it, the Sacrament carries on the servant of God in a fervent desire for all well doing. In all that I say of the Sacrament, I trust the wise reader to understand that it is not this means alone without other means and helps that does this. But rather as the Lord in His great favor to His church has provided a variety of means for His children as their weakness requires, some public and some private, so has He made this one of the various means to promote a godly life.

I thought this was very important to add because, of all the other helps to the practice of Christianity, I am persuaded that the sacraments are the least considered and found to be useful in this way. For the most part they are used without the benefit God has joined to them—that is, only in ceremony, but not to edification. Because this wholesome use of them is so little seen or enjoyed, people either neglect to return to them or approach them with irreverence, disorder, and even profane behavior in the administration and reception of them. This, then, is the principal matter to be regarded and considered concerning the Sacrament, both by the minister and the people.

But it is not my purpose to develop this argument more fully. Seeing that the sacraments do seal God's promises to the faithful receiver under a visible and infallible sign and bind Him (I speak with reverence) to performing His covenant, and seeing that the sacrament of baptism engrafts the believer into Christ, while the Lord's Supper works upon the believer as has been seen (by holy preparation before he comes, with comfort in receiving, and in strengthening him afterward), I conclude therefore that the sacraments are singular helps for all true believers to grow in a godly life. Consequently, whoever is not made more able to conquer his lusts and weaken the strength of sin and is not more encouraged to the life of godliness by the sacraments abuses them and fails to see God's purpose in ordaining them. This sin God will severely punish, as the example of the Corinthians testifies and proves (1 Cor. 11:30).

CHAPTER 3

Public Prayers

The public prayers solemnly offered to God in the congregation and the praising of God with psalms is another of these public helps. And who doubts that we will receive much help through these means, if that mind is in us with which we have been taught to prepare for and come to all holy exercises? Yes, the better a person is, the more profit he will receive by these helps. For when the faithful have a promise from God Himself that they will be heard in all things that are good for them, even the most excellent, and then do empty their hearts by confessing their sins with the rest of the godly and lift their spirits and voices together in praising Him, is there any doubt that they are afterward more cheerfully inclined to serve Him?

How to Profit from Public Prayers

Though the ignorant (which in the best congregations is commonly the greatest number) receive no more profit from public prayers, this is not the fault of the exercises themselves, which are good ordinances, but because the ignorant are unfit to receive benefit from the prayers. The cause of this unfitness arises either from prejudiced opinions (in some) or from ignorance and rash zeal (in others), leading them to a slight and negligent hearing and attending to the prayers.

The direct remedy for these faults, humanly speaking, is an ordinary, able ministry of the word. Through such a ministry, the ignorant might learn (along with other good things) how to rightly use public prayers, while the prejudiced (who think poorly of public prayers, because they see little fruit from them without the word preached) should be silent and have nothing to say against the prayers, so long as both (preaching and public prayers) went together.

But God's children are especially refreshed through public prayers and therefore should hear them as well as the sermon. The Lord Himself has appointed not only private supplications and thanksgivings, but also public prayers, and these in so solemn a manner, with the whole assembly consenting together in the same requests and the Lord present among us to assist us, as He has promised (Matt. 18:20). Public prayers are the very ordinance of God, and He promises a blessing to them as often as we are partakers in them. We will, then, receive fruit from public prayers if we come in true repentance with reverence, a sense of our needs, and an earnest desire and confidence to obtain the things for which we pray.

Objections to Public Prayer Answered

Objection 1. However, since ministers have for the most part been disordered and ignorant persons (as too many still are) and, like the sons of Eli, have brought themselves by God's just judgment and their own deserts into dishonor and discredit, it has come to pass that many through rash judgment have had an evil opinion of the service they have used and have therefore thought they had cause to sequester themselves from being present at the service of God performed by ministers and thus object against it.

Objection 2. Others have thought all set forms of prayer are to be disliked, and that the only prayers to be allowed and offered up to God are those conceived and uttered extemporaneously according to every one's necessity. This opinion is also to be reformed.

I will say something to both objections (though it is not my purpose to discourse of them at length). This I say: that public prayer (as has also been said of preaching and the sacraments) is a great help to godliness to all such as have any measure of godliness. Otherwise, the blame belongs to those who through ignorance and darkness do not know that they ought "to pray always, with all manner of supplications and giving of thanks" and therefore publicly as well as privately, when many hearts are poured out to God, rather than just a few or one alone. If they do know this, then their sin is greater in that they resist and spurn against it.

Answer to Objection 1. Although it is not to be denied that the example of ignorant, unreformed, and especially notorious persons in the ministry have done and continue to do much harm, yet if they either cannot be convicted or if their crimes are such as cannot remove them out of their places, then there is just cause of grief that such men should have anything to do in God's matters, which are so weighty and to be dealt in with all high reverence. Yet, if this burden must be borne, I ask, may we not join in prayer with them, if we can pray in faith, seeing their unworthiness cannot withhold the fruit of God's promise from us? For God's promise is to one kind of prayer as well as to another: "Ask, and ye shall receive, that your joy may be full" (John 16:24). And as it is far from me to justify or be a patron of such men as the true ministers of God, yet while we may enjoy the ministry of better, I would not refuse to be partaker of the prayers offered up by them. Who can blame someone who desires to pray with those who are better? And yet it is better to join with them sometimes than to leave the public assemblies altogether.

Answer to Objection 2. Concerning the second objection, that though the ministers are not as offensive as the former, yet they should not use a set form of prayer but pray only as they are moved by God's Spirit, I answer

that it is a fond error to think this. For as there are necessary things to be prayed for always and by all men,
so prescribed forms of prayer may be made concerning
all such things. If this is so, what hinders the hearers'
hearts from profitably consenting with the reading of
forms of prayer, whether they are prayers of confession
of sins, request, or thanksgiving? What hinders them
from being humbled, quickened, and comforted by these
prayers? For is the reading itself impure when the minister on behalf of himself and the people utters them
to God? I am not speaking about the content of prayer,
but of reading it. For if the content is erroneous, then
the words pronounced do not make it good; and if the
content is good and pure, then the reading cannot make
it evil. The church in Scripture sings (and continues to
sing) psalms out of a book to God, even though it is a
prescribed form of words. I hope none will say that this
is a sin! In like manner, I hope none will say it is a sin to
follow a prescribed form of words in praying, when the
heart is prepared in a similar manner. This should not be
offensive to anyone.

If someone asks how can men daily repeat the
same form of words, as they do in the reading of public
prayer, without being cold and so abominable to God,
I answer that it is not frequently praying for the same
things that is odious to God, but when this is done with
an irreverent, unprepared, and corrupt heart—when it
is done for custom, rather than fervently and in faith.

For do not the best people pray daily for faith, meekness, humility, peace, and such things (seeing we have daily need of them), and yet without weariness? To further satisfy them, they may know that in all churches, even the best reformed churches, there is a prescribed form of prayer used. Therefore, those who are of the mind that this should not be must separate themselves from all churches. Furthermore, if a set form of prayer were unlawful, then even the Lord's Prayer (which is a set form of prayer prescribed by our Savior Himself) should not be used. Now, though the Lord's Prayer is sometimes used in the form in which it is written down, yet I do not think it amiss to add this: that though our Savior tied us to the matter of this prayer as being perfect and full, yet He tied us not to the words themselves, seeing we cannot either think on, remember, or desire in one moment all the specific things contained in those words. And besides, by craving particularly the things we stand in need of, we are more stirred up and moved.

Having answered these objections, I will proceed, persuading all good Christians to lay aside contention as well as endless and often needless questions about this matter. Let them resolve together what must be granted: that public prayers are a help to stir up God's graces in us and to convey to us the many good blessings of God, which we need. Therefore, let all watch themselves carefully to always keep themselves fit to be helped and benefited by them. And with the same well-ordered hearts and minds may they attend and apply to themselves the prayers which are read in their hearing either before or after the sermon. Let them not be led astray by the opinion that they will not profit by these prayers. Neither let them be as many people are, who after going to church for a long time show that they have not benefited by the prayers by not being able to show how they should pray or behave during public prayers. Rather, seeing they have liberty to hear and generously enjoy the preaching of God's word, let them take their part in both the preaching and the public prayers with cheerfulness and thanksgiving.

The Singing of Psalms

In the singing of psalms, those who cannot read should attend to those who are nearest them in the congregation to join with them in praising God with the rest of the assembly. Let them not gaze about or stir up vain imaginations and fantasies, when they should rather lift pure hearts and hands to God (1 Tim. 2:8). As for those who refuse to take part in the worship of God altogether, as the Brownists[1] and others, let them bear their shame before men. Their peace will be small while they sit at home with their own bare reading for their diet and scorn the best liberties of the preached word, prayer, and the sacraments in the public assemblies. For

---

1. The Brownists were early dissenters and separatists from the Church of England, named after Robert Browne (ca. 1550–1633).

so they have confessed before the magistrate that having absented themselves from public meetings for the whole month or quarter, they sat at home and read by themselves. Let all judge by what spirit such are led.

CHAPTER 4

The Necessity of Private Helps

Having explained the nature and use of the public helps, I think it is necessary before dealing specifically with the private helps to say something about their necessity alongside the public means.

Professing Christians Are Less Acquainted with the Private Helps

This is needful because thousands of professing Christians in the visible church (among whom we hope God has many elect) are little acquainted with the private means and think it needless to listen concerning them. In addition, some of God's dear children for lack of teaching show meager use of the private helps and are much the worse for it.

For these causes, therefore, this is to be known and held in firm persuasion: that the private means are as needful as the public. For the private may be used at all times, whereas the public cannot. The private can be used in and throughout the other six days of the week and in times of persecution. And just as our bodies need daily refreshing, so do our souls. Seeing then that the public means cannot be used daily, we must use the private. Both the public and the private are therefore authorized and commanded by God.

The Public Means Are Less Helpful without the Private

Furthermore, the public means are only some of the helps God has provided for the benefit of His church. Therefore, without the private helps, the public are less profitable.

For example, coming to church (the only way many know of serving God) cannot do that good to the best Christians which is to be looked for, if it is not accompanied with the private helps. This may be seen in every part of the public worship of God.

The Ministry of the Word Is Less Helpful without Private Meditation and Reading

This is because hearing the word read and preached does little profit when it is not joined with preparation to hear reverently and attentively and when it is not afterward mused upon or discussed with others (as occasion may offer), and if private reading is not used. What is more manifest than this, that almost everyone in the congregation before long forgets what they have heard and makes little use of it in their lives? And what greater cause can be given for this than that they never attend to matters concerning their souls when they are in private and outside the church doors?

The Lord's Supper Is Less Helpful without Private Preparation

In like manner, what use do such people make of the Lord's Supper? For the most part, they cannot tell how to prepare themselves for it. If some ministers who are more careful over their people's souls than others teach and examine them concerning the knowledge they have, yet they cannot be brought to sincerely examine themselves whether they come in true faith and unfeigned repentance, because for the whole quarter before receiving they are not inclined to trouble themselves about such matters[1]—by this it may be certainly gathered that they lightly esteem those things the Scriptures commend. If they do not privately and carefully nourish these good graces of God in themselves (for I speak of even the better sort of Christians, as well as others) before receiving the Sacrament, who thinks they will bother to willingly examine their hearts in its actual observance?

---

1. Rogers was writing in a context where quarterly observance of the Lord's Supper was common.

Public Prayer Is Less Helpful without Private
Prayer and Family Prayer

We can say the same concerning the public hearing of prayer in the assembly. If they neglect to pray to God alone in secret and in their families, it should not be doubted that they pray in hypocrisy, drawing near to God with their mouths, their hearts being far from Him (Matt. 15:8–9). Not only this, but public prayer also becomes wearisome to them, even a bare ceremony, in those who have not learned to consciously observe private prayer but instead divide the public from the private, contrary to God's ordinance in joining them together.

The Private Helps Should Not Be Neglected

By this it is clear how necessary it is for all who have their part in public means to use the private helps as well.

And not only do our necessities require it but the Lord commands it. He has given time and liberty from our other business and duties, either in family or otherwise, to use these helps in holiness and to continue in them. Our worldly affairs should then give place to the private helps, though many through ignorance count them ridiculous and foolish. Others, though they will not speak so rudely, are so gripped by the world that they give little to no attention to serving God. But it is manifest that where God is best and most purely served, then their earthly business has the best success.

I thought it would be helpful to share these brief thoughts before further discussing the private helps, so that the people who conscientiously practice these helps may not think they are doing more than they should or have need for; so that those who use them slackly and coldly may bestow greater diligence in them; and so that the private helps may be better esteemed among all sorts, if they desire to see good days here upon earth.

CHAPTER 5

Watchfulness

Following the division made of the private helps in the introduction of this treatise, the first private help is watchfulness, which is worthily set in the first place, seeing it is as an eye to all the rest to see them well and rightly used.

The Nature of Watchfulness

Watchfulness is a careful observing of our hearts and diligent looking to our ways, that they may be pleasing and acceptable unto God. First, it is an observing of the heart, as Solomon proves, saying, "Keep thy heart with all diligence; for out of it are the issues of life" (Prov. 4:23). Watchfulness also makes a man look diligently to his ways, as the words of the prophet testify: "I said, I will take heed to my ways, that I sin not with my tongue: I will keep my mouth with a bridle" (Ps. 39:1). And that God is pleased by both is evident by the contrary, for so it is said, "If any man draw back,"—which cannot be without watching—"my soul," says God, "shall have no pleasure in him" (Heb. 10:38). God therefore delights in the opposite.

This is commended in various places in Scripture, that we should have a great care how we live and watch over all our ways. St. Peter says, "Be sober, be vigilant" (1 Peter 5:8). It is as though he says that even if we have sobriety, which is a well ordering of our affections (which is a fit virtue to keep the life in frame), yet without watchfulness, it will be lost. Our Savior joins watchfulness with prayer when He says, "Watch and pray, that ye enter not into temptation" (Matt. 26:41; Mark 13:33). This teaches that the effectiveness of the one is much weakened and abated without the other, and that men will make but cold prayers if they watch not their lives.

Both give their reason why carefully watching over ourselves should be our companion; for without watchfulness, we are before long plunged into many foul temptations by Satan and by our own sinful hearts. The necessity of this one help may also be easily seen in our own experience and by the contrary sin of carelessness. For what grieves and quenches the Holy Spirit of God more easily than anything that chases away godliness? Or what except carelessness so opens the door to confusion?

The Manner of Watchfulness

Furthermore, because of the urgent necessity of watching, St. Paul warns Timothy to watch in all things

(2 Tim. 4:5). Not in just one thing or in few, but in all—and therefore, at all times, in all places, with all persons, and by all occasions. This caused King David, that holy man of God, seeing he could not discharge duty to God without a special regard and taking heed to his life (because of Satan's vigilance), to covenant and profess, "I will behave myself wisely in a perfect way. O when wilt thou come unto me? I will walk within my house with a perfect heart" (Ps. 101:2). And that I may not be thought to speak absurdly because I speak otherwise than most men's practice approves, look at other Scriptures, and you will see this truth more clearly. I must make this foundation strong, seeing there is a great weight to be set upon it. In the third chapter of Hebrews: "Take heed, brethren, lest there be in any of you an evil heart of unbelief" (v. 12). What less can this mean but that from time to time we should look unto and take heed of the heart and its manifold affections and desires, lest the Lord should thereby be offended?

This taking heed therefore to yourself and especially to your heart (because the words and actions come from the heart) must be your companion all the time, and you must set this watch before the door of your lips and be well acquainted with looking diligently to your ways, that it may go with you and that you may prosper. But if you are a stranger to watchfulness, look to fall often—I mean to fall dangerously (for otherwise he that watches most warily cannot be free from offending; even he that watches best sometimes sleeps). Look to find many wounds in your soul and to lack many comforts in your life.

This I may boldly say is why many (and these not evil men) make many jarring mistakes in their lives and break often into unseemly actions and do many things against their holy profession. Before long they cover these things with the gentle name of infirmities, but in truth they willfully fulfill the desires of their hearts and rashly and inordinately indulge themselves, utterly refusing in those cases this holy watchfulness. They view such watchfulness as bondage, as depriving Christians of their liberty, and as too strict. But watching is to the life what the eyelid is to the eye, and what the eye itself is to the whole body. And as it is easily aggravated unless it is carefully and wisely guarded from wind and weather, so it is with your soul and life when you do not take heed to them as you are taught by God's Word and good instruction. For a due looking to your ways is the safety of your life.

The Evil of Neglecting Watchfulness

Because this is seldom welcome to men and little practiced, therefore they are mere strangers to a well-ordered and settled course of life. Instead, because they mostly live in false security, their hearts are out of frame, and their lives are void of good order. For what else can be said when some, such as Nabal (1 Sam. 25:10), are so hot, hasty, and furious for religion that they are not fit to live with? And others, such as Gehazi (2 Kings 5:25), are so hollow and untrustworthy that they cannot be dealt with? Alas, I am weary of so often reprimanding the unreformed qualities and actions of so many who profess to be Christians. And many of them (it may be thought) truly are Christians. And yet, until they recognize this lack of watchfulness and learn to be acquainted with it, they will never be settled but rather will continue to be out and in, off and on.

How a Christian Must Frame Himself to Watchfulness
Those who desire to be helped by watchfulness must purpose to set their mind and delight upon it. They must be content to be dealt with like children, who are not allowed to handle or play with knives; or as the mentally insane, who are kept from occasions to hurt themselves. Thus, as the apostle says, Christians must abstain and wean themselves from their evil lusts which fight against their souls to destroy them. They must not venture into any relationships or conversations that promote evil desires, nor give themselves freedom to fulfill such desires. The prophet said he behaved himself as one weaned from his mother's breast. And as experienced Christians cannot but remember how they were on all occasions vulnerable to danger and stumbling before they became watchful, and since they see how beneficial watchfulness is to them and how it keeps them in safety

on every side, so they will easily discern how badly it goes for all who walk without watchfulness. We must especially practice watchfulness because it is one of the helps that is of greatest value which God has commanded us to use for our daily benefit.

Prayer Must Go with Watching
As our Savior admonishes us, prayer is to go with watchfulness. Prayer quickens watchfulness and puts life into it, causing it to be continued with much cheerfulness and little tediousness, while we prayerfully trust God to bless it unto us. Therefore, He says, "Watch and pray, lest you fall into temptation." His words also point out the time in which we should watch—namely, as long as we are in danger of being tempted or drawn to sin. But many Christians, having not weighed the danger, think watching deprives them of too much freedom and therefore refuse to be guided by this teaching. But with good advice, those who will not be contentious will easily see the value of what has been said about this matter.

The Necessity of Watchfulness
I thank God that I have known many godly Christians who have found the fruit of watchfulness so sweet that they would not omit it again. When they were first urged to watch and before they had experience in it, they argued against it. They did not like having the things they had done in rashness, haste, and without good advice being brought into question. But having

now found such great gain in it, they would not for any reason return to their former rashness and false security.

Watchfulness Is Counted Too Strict until People Are Well Acquainted with It

I do not doubt that many to whom God has given some taste and savor in heavenly things may lacking experience at first think the urging of this watching to be overly strict. Yet after further insight into it, as being both commanded by God and of singular gain, they will see their error and rather than holding to their former judgment will pray most earnestly to have their part in it. I speak not as though any who fear God were mere strangers to this grace and gift of God, for I know they are not without it sometimes. But I speak of those who have not resolved in their judgment that they should watch at all times, or of those who have too much neglected it.

The Answer to Those Who Say They Cannot Watch

Some object that they cannot be as mortified as some believers are, or always observing themselves the way believers do, but should rather be content with their current level of godliness. But this is unfitting for Christians who should be growing in watchfulness, as in all other kinds of grace. And yet I count their case better than those who think they can serve God without all this effort. After all, they pray and go to church; so why should they examine the rest of their behavior or take heed to the same? Regardless of how such people please themselves, it is sure that they resist God. It is to be greatly lamented that those who profess the gospel should have so little benefit from this gracious help, which is so often preached to them.

See to it that you (whoever you are) who desire to walk with God in peace look circumspectly to your steps and the various affections of your heart. Consider how you carry yourself and how you should endeavor to watch in all things. This is to be marked and learned, because it lends help to all the other rules that follow for directing you in all the actions of your daily life.[1] For you cannot please God in company or in solitude, in prosperity or in adversity, unless you are led by God's Word to be wary and watchful. This virtue is so necessary to the Christian that the apostle Paul warns the Ephesians that when they have put on the whole armor and have withstood the enemy by it, they are to take heed that they stand fast, lest by the subtle and persistent attention of the enemy their fall is greater (cf. Eph. 6:13). This can easily be the case if we consider the many occasions and provocations to sin through which we walk, how careless we are to avoid them, and how quick we are to yield to them.

---

1. Rogers further expounds the rules for governing daily life in the fourth book of *Seven Treatises*. See page 68, footnote 1 below.

The Motives for Watchfulness

We are burdened with evil desires, which carry us headlong into various iniquities. We can do nothing without feeling that one or another of these desires is out to hurt us and at hand to molest and trouble us. Or, if we cannot see this in the moment, we can at least see this in hindsight.

On one side, shame and hypocrisy are there to hinder us when we are occupied in holy and spiritual duties. Dullness, weariness, reluctance, and many other poisoned corruptions are there on the other side to break us off. When engaged in lawful and indifferent things, which are not evil in themselves, such as recreation or earthly business, we are careless in how we do them. And we are bold to defend ourselves no matter how vain and evil our manner and purpose. Then, the promise of pleasure and profit of sin persuades us to go through with evil actions. We rationalize our sin rather than seeing the danger that accompanies it and looking, as we should, to its outcome (Eccl. 8:11). But all sound reason to dissuade us from evil is weak. The devil shows himself at such times as a tempter; but afterward, when we should repent, he comes as an accuser.

Therefore, if we are not skillful in knowing these disordered desires and diligent to observe, prevent, and avoid them so as to have this watchfulness over our lives, it cannot be otherwise that we will commit many things unbecoming to us and contrary to the holy doctrine we profess to follow. This will be so in many things throughout the whole course of our lives. And when someone is thus carried along by his disordered affections and brings forth their loathsome fruit, what comfort can his life bring? All those who refuse to curtail their foolish, vain desires and consider it a death to withdraw their hearts and pluck their eyes back from the object of their sinful delights and desires will feed upon emptiness and take comfort in folly. But they are strangers to the healthy, constant joy of those who have made a watchful life their greatest peace and therefore have the liberty and capacity to solace their souls in heavenly pleasures.

When One Is Not Watchful, One Trial Makes Many Blessings Distasteful
By watchfulness, the Lord has freely granted us to find and enjoy a manner of living in this world that is different than most know, that is a peaceful, Godward life, that is both safe and sweet—I mean, so far as sinners need in this vale of misery. Whoever lacks this, even though they have a variety of earthly pleasures and delights, yet one vexing trial will make their comforts tiresome and distasteful. This is seen in Pharaoh, when just one of the plagues of Egypt came upon him (Exodus 8); and in Nebuchadnezzar, when he had his fearful dream (Daniel 2); and in Belshazzar, when in the midst of his merriness he saw at midnight the fearful and

unwelcome handwriting on the wall (Daniel 5). Among all these examples, this is nowhere more evident than in Haman, who for all his wealth, honor, and power could not be satisfied as long as one obscure man, even a stranger, Mordecai, refused to bow to him.

Or to use an example of someone who had more knowledge of the true God, the same can be said of Saul. Even though he was a king, yet when the Lord answered him no longer, his heaviness was deadly (1 Samuel 28). This is also seen in Nabal. When he heard he must die, he became senseless through sorrow and anguish and was as a stone (ch. 25). Or consider Zedekiah, who despite all his boasting of the Spirit of God yet being a false prophet and a flatterer was driven to hide himself from chamber to chamber (1 Kings 22) when Micaiah told him that the arrow of the Lord was sent against him and the king's shelter could not keep him. In all these examples, just one disturbance in life made all other delights unpleasant.

Therefore, I may truly say, as the life which is passed in watchfulness is free from many (and those also the greatest) discomforts and is filled with the contrary peace, so whatever a man enjoys according to his heart's desire, yet if he looks not to his ways to keep himself from evil, fear and sorrow will ever befall him (unless he is hardened, which is worse). His life will have little cause for joy.

How the Best People Have Offended When
They Have Not Been Watchful

The reason for urging the Christian duty of continual watching may be seen in the example of our grand-mother Eve (1 Tim. 2:14). Though she was in the state of innocence and therefore more likely to have been kept from evil, yet because she was not watchful and vigilant in holding close to God's command she became the cause of transgression to her husband, which led to the universal misery of her posterity.

We see the same thing in the example of King David. Though as renowned and commended as any man in Scripture for his meditation on the law of God, yet since he was not armed with a watchful heart when he walked on the roof of his palace (2 Sam. 11:2), behold how the devil baited him. Though David was wise, he did not discern and was ensnared by the devil's subtle and secret ways. He then received such recompense for letting loose his heart at that time, both in outward reproach and inward anguish and bitterness of soul, that others have good reason to cleave fast to watchfulness and be faithful to the Lord. Yes, they should beware with all diligence that they dally not with the baits of sin nor give their hearts free rein, lest they go so far that they cannot be called back again before committing great offense.

My own long experience in teaching both myself and others the necessity and benefit of a watchful course makes me even more bold and earnest in persuading those who have sincerely embraced the gospel to join this godly watch to their faith. It will nourish and strengthen their faith. Believers should settle themselves in this watch wherever they go and whatever they do: that their talk is not idle, but savored with salt; that their actions are such as commend a peaceful conscience against their accusers; and that they labor to subdue even their wicked thoughts and desires, weakening the body of sin itself, that is, the old man with his lusts.

Other Gifts Are Beautified by Watchfulness

Even among those who rejoice in the testimony of a good conscience and who most honor the gospel, the ones who most stop the mouth of the gainsayer are those who carry themselves most constantly and continually in an even and good course, who have been wise in this way, and who have determined to watch at all times. On the other hand, those (both among teachers and hearers) who may be praised in many good things yet are noted for being rash and unstable in their actions, who fail to watch and govern themselves, have done less good to others by their example and have caused their good qualities to be less regarded.

God be glorified for the good that is done in many through watchfulness. But if this watchfulness were more commonly embraced by those who are able to give light to others, then they would not be most in disgrace who least deserved it. Nor would many please themselves in a loose and unprofitable way of living, which hinders their comfort and is a sore blemish in their lives.

I should add this: while those in the Roman Church who seem to be more devout than others and stand much upon their diligence in keeping the customs of their mother church and the precepts of men might seem to themselves and others to be greater in godliness, let everyone know that what I have said about watchfulness leaves them no commendation. For they watch to keep the observances of men, but watchfulness must be used for obeying the commandments of God. They watch superstitiously to observe hours, days, and times; and in these outward performances think themselves more holy than others, even though other times are but little regarded. But the watchfulness which pleases God attends to *every* hour, day, and time—one as well as another. And the best watch they keep over their lives is not allowed by God, because from their own words we can conclude that it does not come from faith—that is, an assurance of God's favor. Therefore, He will not bless it; for without this faith (which they call the Protestant faith and utterly renounce) it is impossible to please God (Heb. 11:6).

We Must Especially Watch against the Infirmity
Which Most Annoys Us

True Christians, even God's dearest servants, complain of special infirmities, which they find themselves more troubled with than any other. They must therefore be more vigilant against those infirmities than others. The devil also leads them into some sins more easily than others, since he sees their disposition and inclination and thus the greater danger they are in. Therefore, they are taught in wisdom and experience to keep a close eye on these infirmities and to especially avoid the occasions where they have fallen in the past.

For example, some are strongly tempted to the sin of uncleanness. But being blind regarding their desires, they think it no offense to cross boundaries regarding lustful eyes, loose speech, or secret desires. They know they are snared in this sin. But through long-standing habits they nourish their hearts in these loathsome delights; and when they become aware of their offenses, they do not dislike them enough. Thus, they have brought themselves in bondage to their lusts.

The heart should therefore be much engaged in fighting against this sin and in observing and weighing its depravity, shame, and danger. They must heartily acknowledge the sin to God and daily offer earnest prayers to God against it, with confidence in both pardon and power to mortify and weaken it. They must use strong reasons to disgrace and renounce the sin. And they must wisely and watchfully avoid the occasions of nourishing the sin. If they do not do this, then this one sin (even if they do not offend grossly) will hold their conscience in great distress, cause them to wander in deep sorrow, and make them unfit for Christian duties. Indeed, if they do not bestow more labor here than in other parts of their lives, it will slow down their progress and cause disorder and confusion to grow. The longer they have nourished such vain dreams, the more difficult will it be to awake out of them, even if they gladly would. And the same can truly be said of other sins as well when they have been harbored.

This is why the people of Israel in their repentance complained that one sin troubled them more than others. For so they confessed that which they had sinned against the Lord, especially in asking for a king (1 Sam. 12:19). And as it most troubled them when they sought pardon from God, so it appears in the story that of all other sins they were most drawn to offend God by this one. When Samuel was sent from God to tell them the kind of king they would get if they sought one against God's will, it is expressly said that the people would not hear the voice of Samuel, but answered, "Nay; but we will have a king over us; that we also may be like all the nations" (8:19–20). Therefore, as their sin which most offended God put them to greatest trouble, so must those same sins which have prevailed against God's children be most watched against and avoided.

Is there not good reason for us to bend our greatest strength against those sins which have most troubled us? Just as a town would expend all their effort to remove and keep out one troublesome person who upset the whole town, and just as we would more quickly fix a chimney filling a well-furnished house with smoke than we would fix other problems in the house, so it is in the lives of healthy Christians. Though there are many good blessings of God to be reaped and enjoyed, the chief ruins must be considered. Even though we should not neglect lesser sins, we must give greater effort to watching against the sin that most prevails in us—more than against those in which there is less danger to be feared.

If this help as I have explained it is used and the means faithfully practiced at all times, let no one doubt that they will conquer it and find peace. For God has promised success and greater grace in the use of this help than sin will be able to resist. In the case of unmarried persons, remember God has also appointed marriage as a lawful remedy for when the gift of continence can no longer be enjoyed (1 Cor. 7:2, 9).

This advice will not be welcomed by those who are married to their lusts and refuse to offer violence against them. But those who know the pain raised by this sin and who know that sometimes God's dear servants have been deceived by it will be glad to be directed and helped against it. And what I have said of uncleanness may also be said of pride, worldliness, anger, malice, revenge, unjust dealing, and lying. Every man should more continually fear and watch against whichever sin most easily overcomes him and hurts him. He should give more time to rooting out that sin than to others. When the most putrid wounds that impair a person are cured, the whole body is better preserved.

But if men be either ignorant of this duty or cannot be persuaded to set themselves considering it and becoming acquainted with it, they should expect to be destitute in a chief aspect of godliness. Or if they are haphazard in regarding the various aspects of their lives (as is the case for those not greatly experienced in Christian practice), then the godly life will be greatly bereft of both benefit and beauty.

Our hearts must not wander where they will, nor must our delights be fastened wherever we please. Our eyes, tongues, ears, hands, feet, the full force of our minds and thoughts, and all the members of our bodies must be bound within limits. If we see that we have faltered out of the way even a little and our consciences begin to check us, we should tremble to think what we have done, always fearing for the time to come, lest we should offend (Prov. 28:14; Phil. 2:12). We must watch when we are well in order to stay well. And when we have been deceived, we must speedily return. When in trouble, we must watch against tiredness and impatience. When in prosperity, we must watch against lust and vanity (Job 31:1).

If we can make this our frame of mind, we will do well, just as he who watches his foot in slippery places is less likely to be hurt. And if by watching over ourselves we may have our whole life in safety and welfare, do we not deserve to hurt when we refuse to do so much for such a great benefit? Those who will not take heed to their ways but cry out that it is too precise and a kind of death to be restrained from dangerous liberties well deserve to suffer hardness and sorrow. For from this spirit arise boldness and stubbornness, leading to much sin. But God requires this watchfulness in us. We should not consider it tedious but cultivate it at any price. Whoever submits himself to this with an honest heart and a good conscience will be able to prove by experience that watchfulness is a great means to maintaining a godly life.

CHAPTER 6

Meditation

The second private help for godliness is meditation.

The Nature of Meditation

We meditate when we purposely separate ourselves from everything else to consider (as we are able) some necessary points of instruction to lead us forward to the kingdom of heaven, to better strengthen us against the devil and this present evil world, and to help us order our lives well. I say "purposely" because we must attend such things under good counsel and resolutely set ourselves to them when we begin. This is necessary if we intend to do them with more reverence and profit. For we seldom enter into meditation of heavenly things unless we intend to do so, but are rather led amiss in a hundred ways by our eyes, cares, and thoughts. Even when good thoughts arise, they are quickly repelled and go no further. Therefore, when we meditate we ought to separate ourselves both from other people and potential distractions, as our Savior commanded when He said we should pray in secret (Matt. 6:6) (since prayer and meditation are companions). We will meditate better when we are alone, whether privately in our room, in the field, or in some other place. The smallest distractions can quickly pull us away from such service to God. Therefore, we must warily avoid them.

Lastly, we must then set our minds to work in thinking about heavenly things by calling to remembrance some truth that we know and then by reasoning about the same, so that our affections are moved to an appropriate response (whether love, delight, hatred, or fear) to the object of our meditation.

The Use of Meditation

In this way, we will make meditation useful to ourselves. This spiritual exercise of meditation is the practice that puts life and strength into all other duties and aspects of worshiping God. This the Holy Spirit reported of the patriarch Isaac, that he went out into the field "to meditate" in the evening (Gen. 24:63). Isaac was commended for his meditation, having been taught by his father Abraham, who was "the friend of God" and therefore no doubt had much communion with God. This was also true of our father Enoch, who is said to have "walked with God" his entire life. Meditation is thus a holy duty which should be often used.

All who desire to benefit from meditation must know this: that they must be thoroughly acquainted with sweet and heavenly communion with both the Lord and themselves. Communion with one's self was called by our ancient fathers their "soliloquy"—that is, their self-talk when alone with the Lord. Just as the weary desire rest, so we who are often troubled and distracted by the variety of business in this world should seek to ease our minds by meditation.

Sometimes we muse and think upon many good things. We ponder our words and actions to be sure they are right. This is not the kind of meditation I have in mind, but rather watchfulness by which we cautiously regard ourselves and take heed to all our ways, as discussed in the previous chapter. Watchfulness is a kind of meditation, for the prophet says, "O how love I thy law! it is my meditation all the day" (Ps. 119:97). And in Joshua: "Thou shalt meditate therein [in the book of the law] day and night" (1:8). We know such meditation could not be free from intermission from people, business, or other actions. It refers rather to their whole course of watchful care over their lives according to the Word.

The Matter of Meditation

The matter of our meditation can be any part of the following:

- God's Word
- God Himself

- His wisdom, power, or mercy
- The infinite variety of good things we receive of His free bounty
- His works and judgments
- Our own estate
- Such as our sins
- The vileness of our corruption that we yet carry with us
- Our mortality
- The changes in this world
- Our deliverance from sin and death
- The manifold afflictions of this life, and how we may in the best way endure them and benefit from them
- The many great privileges we enjoy every day through God's inestimable kindness toward us
- And, especially those things which we have most special need of

These and similar things are the matter of our meditation; and as often as we go aside to think with purpose and desire upon any of these things to better call our minds out of the world, then we are said to meditate.

When we sigh, moan, complain to God, or rejoice, and are quickened in our hearts about any of these things, that also is meditation. Usually it is joined with prayer. The book of Psalms is full of these two holy exercises, especially Psalm 119, where the man of God sets down the meditations he had in every state—including lamentation, complaint, supplication in affliction, joy, and giving thanks for deliverances and for prosperity.

So this is the manner of exercising meditation. This exercise is required of us throughout life. And this is how you do it: by recording holy and divine things, especially those which may make you sound in the matter of your salvation. And this you do to give time to mortifying earthly mindedness and worldliness and to quicken your dull heart, lest by sleeping in sin the devil make you forget your formerly well-ordered life.

Too few are acquainted with meditation, even though it is a beneficial help to godliness. My hope is that the practice of meditation will become more common among believers and that those who use it with the other helps may live with more joy.

The Necessity of Meditation

The necessity of this heavenly exercise may be easily conceived for the hearts of even good Christians (for the best are only partially changed and reformed), who are so seasoned with unsavory thoughts, desires, and vain, foolish delights that they think it utterly impossible to bring their hearts to a better place. Because of this error, many do expend no great effort in meditation. Yet if such annoying poisons are suffered to lurk and remain in their hearts, they are like bitter weeds that not only choke the plants of grace but also bring forth harmful, dangerous fruits. This by woeful experience is felt and known.

Meditating to Fight Sin

There is no better means available for weeding the sins from the ground of our hearts than deeply meditating on our sins as the swarms of wicked thoughts and lusts that lodge in the heart, so as to discover them, bring them to account, be weary and ashamed of them, and replace them with better thoughts. This is the best help for purging our sins, because we not only know our sins through the Word but also by conference we revive the memory of them (Heb. 2:1), and by reading do both. Yet these truths leak from our split heads and feebly abide with us. But we must suppress our corruption and tame our hearts until we bring ourselves to frequent and abundant meditation on the good things we hear and read, so that we may digest them. And just as worldly men deeply ponder their weighty business, so we must consider the evils which we do by occasion fall into, so that we may abandon them.

The only way to break up these cursed swarms and chase away from our hearts the lurking litter of ungodly thoughts and desires is to so clearly see their danger that we are wearied by them and thus frequently test ourselves. We test ourselves to gauge our hearts and sift our thoughts, accusing and condemning those thoughts which are filthy and shameful. If we love our souls, we will deal honestly with ourselves. This will make us more watchful against them afterward, as we combine this with earnest requests to God for His help and blessing. In so doing, we graciously furnish our hearts with heavenly thoughts and holy desires, which greatly help us live better lives. Holy meditation on our estate and on God's bounty toward us frames us after God's image. And this works great things in our hearts. No one who weighs this should doubt now the necessity of meditation.

The Deceitfulness of Our Hearts

We have even more to think this way, because we know from Scripture and experience that the heart is deceitful above all things (Jer. 17:9). We must keep ourselves in check. Even when we commend what is good and condemn what is evil, and so are we ready to think our estate is good (Rom. 2:28), we can deceive ourselves. If we do not by secret meditation search our thoughts in solitude so that we may feel sincere hatred of evil and love for goodness, we deceive ourselves. In every little trial, we will discover that sin even clings to us more than we first imagined.

We Must Set against Our Sin in Our Private Meditation, before We Can Cast It Off in Public

Before someone goes to war, he is first trained to use his weapons. In the same way, the student masters his studies in private before he openly debates. In the same way, a good Christian must fight against his affections and sins in solitary meditation before he can stand against temptations and be free from offense in his words and deeds in daily life among other people. The reason why so many betray themselves to be hypocrites is because they do not test the sincerity of their hearts alone by themselves in testing and proving their uprightness of their hearts before God (Rom. 2:28–29), and so have not asked Him for strength against their infirmities.

The Sweet Benefit of Meditation

Oh, how this secret communion with the Lord and this reflection on our mortality and corruption and God's favor in vanquishing them, how this softens our hard hearts and affects them with sweetness! When we separate ourselves from worldly hindrances, it draws us into closer communion with God. It acquaints us with the various rebellions of our fallen nature: our blindness, earthliness, false security, and other corruptions, which we would otherwise never know. Who would ever think that so much poison could be enclosed in the narrow space of one foolish person's heart?

Oh, the great fruit and benefit we reap from meditation and private prayer! By these means the Spirit of God changes our hearts from their old ways and brings us into more affinity with the heavenly life. That which the men of this world find so irksome and distasteful, the Spirit makes easier and sweeter to our souls. This fruit is so great that no one can conceive it until they have felt it. For by this God keeps the sugared baits of earthly delights and the transitory pleasures of the world from becoming a deadly poison to us. Though Satan kindles in us an excessive and inordinate love of these things, the Lord teaches us to see through their façade and deception and helps us to see them for what they are and thus be wary of them.

The Scripture notes how the men of God most commended for their piety, such as Moses, David, Paul, and others, were devoted to meditation. I boldly dare to affirm therefore that the godliest people in our time may also thank God much for their acquaintance with meditation and their frequent use of it. Others who are strangers to meditation, no matter how wise they are in other practices of Christian duty, would be much more purged and cleansed from evil if alongside their other services to God they were acquainted with meditation joined with private prayer (this secret talking with God and with their own hearts).

Meditation Is a Stranger to Many
Though I do not expect to persuade profane people (who are addicted and given over to the full enjoyment of their heart's desire in this present world) to regard this practice of meditation, yet my hope is to easily prevail with those who are ready and willing to do well if they are only taught. I want them to highly esteem meditation because of the close acquaintance with God which they may gain by it, as they are enabled. But the

truth is, even people of good hope who are unaccustomed to meditation will find it new and strange—so much so that when they hear from the Word of God that it is a duty required by God, they are ready to argue against it as something too difficult. Even though meditation would benefit them greatly, they are content to serve God without it, instead of immediately embracing it. That is why they need to see the necessity, benefit, and possibility of it. We have now shown how necessary and beneficial meditation is. In the next section, we will consider the hindrances to meditation and the remedies against them. Following that, I will show how possible, even how easy, meditation will in time become. From this, the benefit and fruit of meditation will be seen.

Three Hindrances to Meditation

Before I speak of the various hindrances to meditation, I am confident by God's assistance that what I say can make meditating so easy and plain for true Christians that the difficulties and discouragements that most trouble them will be removed, or at least weakened. No matter what the causes are why some people fail to benefit from this help, I will show them the way in a few pages. With just a few weeks of practice, they can learn how to benefit from meditation. Otherwise, those without help could be void of this benefit for many years.

There are two sorts of impediments that hold God's people strangers from using meditation with benefit.

Some of these hinder them from meditating at all. The other impediments are abuses of meditation, which keep people from benefiting from the practice, even though they set other things aside that they may devote time to it. Of the former sort, there are three.

Lack of Matter for Meditation
The first hindrance is when a Christian knows this duty is required of him and goes about it either in the morning (as I think he should) or another convenient time, but has no matter ready to meditate upon. He is empty and barren. He is at a loss for knowing how to spend his time and fix his thoughts. Even though he has heard many things in sermons that he could meditate upon and benefit from, and even though he carries with him many corruptions and has received many blessings and mercies from God, yet the devil holds him. He is blind and forgetful. His mind is confused and occupied with other things, so that he finds nothing to muse upon by which to season his heart.

When he sees that he then cannot proceed in the duty he has been taught to perform, even though he desires to do so, he is very discouraged. His heart is heavy, and this makes him less persuaded to try to meditate. He finds himself unable to ask for help. For those who are ensnared and outmatched by the devil will hardly seek a remedy if anything is amiss with them. Instead, they quit trying altogether. This behavior is opposite to the children of this world, who when they are disappointed in their purposes are wise enough to attempt other ways to fulfill their desires (see Luke 16:2–3, 8).

The remedy for this hindrance, lest any weak Christian should find himself unable to sufficiently direct himself (and until he is better able to go further on his own), is to muse upon these four things:

(1) His unworthiness, vileness, various corruptions, and sins.

(2) The greatness of God's bounty in forgiving his many sins and daily subduing, more and more, the dominion of sin and Satan within him.

(3) He should be guided through the present day after the rules of his daily direction[1]

---

1. Rogers lists and explains these rules in the fourth treatise. For example, in chapter 8, Rogers includes the following list of daily goals or directions:

1. That every day we should be humbled for our sins, as through due examination of our lives by the law of God we will see them.

2. That every day we be raised up in assured hope of the forgiveness of them, by the promises of God in Christ.

3. That every day we prepare our hearts "to seek the Lord" still, and keep them fit and willing thereto.

4. That every day we strongly and resolutely arm ourselves against all evil and sin, fearing most of all to offend God.

5. That every day we nourish our fear and love of Him, and joy in Him more than in any thing, and endeavor to please

(especially those which seem hardest to follow) as he seeks to both rightly order his heart and frame his life in agreement with God's Word.

Him in all duties, as occasion will be offered, looking for His coming (2 Thess. 3:5).

6. That every day our thanks be continued for benefits received, and still certainly hoped for.

7. That every day "we watch and pray" for steadfastness and constancy in all these.

8. That every day we hold and keep our peace with God, and so lie down with it.

If the various spiritual disciplines (or "helps") were the warp, these daily directions were the woof in the pursuit of godliness. For while the helps functioned as practical habits of body and mind for cultivating a godly life, the directions supplied the heart-oriented goals—i.e., humility, assurance, resolution against sin, the fear and love of God, gratitude, steadfastness, and peace—to be sought in such endeavors. As Rogers says, "And this is the direction which every Christian must practice every day in his life, and these are the necessary parts of it, which may not be omitted any day at all without sin: nor carelessly and wittingly without great sin." These kinds of daily directions would be further developed, expanded, and popularized by later Puritan authors, such as Lewis Bayly's *The Practice of Piety* (c. 1611), John Downame's *A Guide to Godliness* (1622), Henry Scudder's *The Christian's Daily Walk* (1631), and Richard Baxter's comprehensive magnum opus, *The Christian Directory* (1673). For further study on these manuals, see Charles Hambrick-Stowe, *The Practice of Piety: Puritan Devotional Disciplines in Seventeenth-Century New England* (Chapel Hill: University of North Carolina Press, 1982).

(4) Let him meditate on the several pieces of the Christian armor, considering how God has appointed this to strengthen him.

Along with this, let him consider the other helps which are to be daily used. These will help him make better progress and will make his life sweeter in many respects. Lastly, let him resolve to watch against all the hindrances which may keep him from following this course.

When he has nothing more necessary to meditate upon, and when he goes about this in the best manner possible as he is directed by an able counselor, these subjects will be a special remedy to help the Christian who otherwise would neglect meditation for lack of matter to meditate upon. These meditations will help him make progress. For anyone who is a true believer, no matter how weak he may be, is still suited (if he is willing) to follow this direction and counsel.

Unfitness for Meditation

The next impediment that hinders a Christian from meditating is an unfit mind for spiritual and heavenly duties, such as when it is slow and unwilling to be occupied with thinking on holy matters because it is carried after other desires. This so hinders the Christian that he finds himself utterly unable to begin meditation. He knows that he should meditate and perhaps is sometimes grieved for omitting it. But if his mind is impotent, having temporarily lost its former strength and constancy in good things, it is constrained to omit meditation and let it pass. Now to rectify this, I answer that if he who omitted it for this reason because of the stubbornness of his heart and his unfitness for good duties be someone who has learned and resolved to daily serve God, he can hardly bear this disorder of heart and will therefore fight it and quickly seek a remedy. But if he has not yet obtained such self-discipline but does his duty to God in a general way, seldom and uncertainly, then he needs even more help. For it is manifest that such a person has given his mind liberty to wander in the world and away from the Christian path.

The remedy to each, as they can receive it, is the same. But it is not necessarily as easy for one as the other. Yet seeing that both belong to the Lord, let them bring their minds to these considerations and say to themselves:

> I have a received a mind to please God (Col. 1:10; Heb. 13:18) and to be teachable and ready for any duty. I have set myself in opposition to my own will and the devil's secret, malicious counsel, even though it is sweet to the flesh. I am not a debtor to the flesh (Rom. 8:12). How then can I yield to this stubbornness of heart and so sin against my God? Where are the many and comfortable privileges God has given me that I might be faithful to Him? Am I weary of my peace? Do I haste after my own sorrow? Lord, bring back, therefore,

this wandering heart of mine from its deceitful dreams, fears, and doubts that have ensnared it. Restore to me the liberty I once enjoyed (Ps. 51:12)—that is, to solace myself in Thy favor and enjoy communion with Thee. May I count it my greatest happiness to fellowship with Thee whenever I may. This gift has decayed through my own fault and the cruelty and subtlety of Satan. Restore me and forgive my cold, weak love for Thee. I have provoked (if Thou hast chosen to be provoked) Thy majesty to frown upon me and look no longer amiably upon me. But Thou hast charged me to seek Thy face, even Thy sweet presence, which I have departed from and have been blinded to, as one having no ability to muse upon anything good. I did not see that I was seduced, until I perceived my loss of sweet liberty. Now therefore, O Lord, show Thy lovingkindness in my distress and weakness, and restore to me this liberty of my heart, which many of Thy children find and enjoy.

This is how to consider yourself. Do not be discouraged when you see your infirmities. You have learned to use your needs to humble yourself and to bring you nearer to God, rather than going further from Him because of them. I conclude therefore that the best remedy for such a person who through an unsettled heart cannot meditate on any parts of Christianity and godliness is to mediate on his present unfitness, looseness of heart, and earthly-mindedness, to count them as a heavy burden, and to accuse his heart and bring it to relent by considering how far off it is from the mildness, humility, heavenliness, and fitness for duty, which had characterized him at other times. But no one should give any kind of liberty to his evil heart when it is turned away from cheerfully and willingly moving forward in any part of God's service, for that will bring him into utter bondage. This is how to address the second hindrance.

Lack of Time and Opportunity for Meditation

The third hindrance is lack of time and opportunity for meditation, since other necessary business takes all their time. In addition, some people (such as seamen or those who must leave their homes) lack a convenient place where they can go for solitude. When they would practice meditation, they either have no room in which to retreat, or they are busy with children or are otherwise surrounded by people. This is often the case in poor families, especially in larger cities.

I do not deny that many, especially those who are occupied with many things, are hindered by necessary business. But I exhort them to weigh their affairs and remember that "one thing is needful" (Luke 10:42). The ordinary duties of their callings must not displace the duty of meditation. If they do, it is because of their stubbornness or lack of skill; for one duty is appointed by God to go with the other, and both stand together for the upholding of their inward peace. If they say they are hindered by more extraordinary works, I further beseech them by the mercifulness of God not to seek cloaks for their sloth nor to hold themselves back from such beneficial duties by occasions of no great weight or importance (but rather for yielding to the flesh). A necessary business is an occasion of great weight when omitting it (even if it is a household duty or worldly affair) will trouble them more than will omitting meditation. For meditation may be performed at another time, while sometimes one's business cannot. Neglecting necessary work through lack of discretion and taking heed when it should be done (and then in the meanwhile engaging in prayer, reading, meditation, or other duties) often troubles the mind with such deep grief because of the disadvantage that results. Then the mind is not quiet and free to serve God. And seeing that God requires us to honor Him in all things, not only in spiritual but also in earthly things, we should not therefore assume that it pleases Him to do something once (through zeal without knowledge) that will quench our zeal for good duties many times thereafter. No one should take the liberty from this to indulge in worldliness.

So, if anyone through necessary hindrances is constrained to skip the duty of meditation when otherwise he would have done it, he should know that it is necessarily skipped. He is without fault, as long as he returns to the duty of meditation after his necessary labor has ended and is careful not to omit it altogether (or unless, in omitting meditation, he is assured and at peace that he has remembered God in some other way). Nothing is to be gained by neglecting those worldly affairs on which our peace and welfare depend.

Two Abuses of Meditation

The other impediments are those that prevent us from using meditation in a profitable way. Though we may break through the previous three hindrances, there are also two abuses of meditation to consider.

Going through the Motions

The first abuse is seen when we are persuaded that meditation must be continued, but we treat it lightly and make a ceremony of it, going through motions without considering whether our hearts are affected. We do this so that we will not be charged with omitting it altogether. This sin is also easily committed in private prayer and other similar exercises, when our minds are not captivated by delight in the duties. This is the reason why most people worship and serve God only for fashion. Of such people God says through the prophet Isaiah, "In vain they do worship me" (Isa. 29:13; Matt. 15:9).

Distracted, Wandering Minds

The second abuse is seen when we desire to use meditation for our help and edification, but our heads are so full of trifling, wandering fantasies and worldly concerns that we cannot "mind those heavenly things," which are so contrary to our thoughts. This leads to weariness in meditation and hurrying through them, so that our hearts can freely wander where they want to—for this is what we most desire. Even the best of God's children complain that they do not do the good they want. Therefore, sometimes they do not do this good (meditation), though they dislike that this is so and resist it. But there is another cause behind this bitterness and weariness in meditation, such a holy and heavenly part of worshiping God. And it is this: when during the day we often let loose our hearts in a disordered way without watching over them and calling them back from such endless wandering. But we must call our hearts back from forgetting God and hold our hearts within bounds, wherever we are and whatever we do, lest there ever be within us an evil heart (Heb. 3:12).

This is the reason why we find it difficult to reverently attend upon God in meditation and prayer when we would. If we have allowed them to attach our hearts to other desires throughout the day, it is hard for us to wean them when the time comes for meditation. As long as we are at this point, we will never improve in meditation, even though God has appointed it as a special help for rightly framing our lives and bringing our minds into a heavenly condition. Yes, even if we appoint special times for meditation, we will be turned from musing on good things to wandering thoughts and will find it difficult to fasten our minds on anything good. Even though we have certain principal points concerning our spiritual condition to begin meditating on, our many trifling fantasies will swim in our brains and hinder us.

Until these are gradually dried up with the flame of heavenly and fervent affection, thus possessing our hearts, it will never be otherwise. We will grow worse and worse. We should wonder at this, seeing that none of our actions can be done well when our hearts are not good and are not preserved and kept by watchfulness. We should wonder, I say, that we are so careless and negligent in keeping our hearts from such danger to ourselves and others, when we know what will result.

Therefore, as the Lord by His prophets cried out against the people in different ages that they perished because they would not understand nor consider their estate (Ps. 49:11–14), and as their deceptive delights will come to an end, although they cannot be brought to think of their end and account—so He speaks as plainly that although in the world we will "have tribulation" (John 16:33), even we whom God has chosen out of the world (15:19), yet seeing "we are strangers here" we cannot neither may we place our heart's delight and happiness here. Rather, our chief comfort must be in daily communion with God and having our conversation in heaven with Him (Phil. 3:20). Meditation is a singular help in this; and whatever weighty matters we busy ourselves with, yet we must "remember our Maker" in them all, that we may please and trust in Him.

Four Rules for Meditation

Now that we have covered the necessity and benefits of meditation, along with the hindrances to it, in what follows I will help the reader with some rules to better guide him in meditating, until the practice becomes more familiar to him (then he will practice meditation better than all rules can teach).

I have already had occasion to mention some of these rules in other places, but have not listed them together for the reader to easily see. Here, therefore, I will list them together.

Rule 1. The first rule is that whoever desires to benefit from meditating should consider how slippery, fickle, bad, wandering, and infinite are the ways of his heart (Jer. 17:9), and how this leads to his exceeding harm. Therefore, he must necessarily appoint a set time to check, reclaim, and wean his heart from these ways.

Rule 2. The second rule is to watch over his heart (Prov. 4:21–23), since he has so often been deceived by it. This he must do throughout his whole life, holding his own heart in suspicion, so that it may be more fit to be drawn and remain in such heavenly exercises. Attend to this.

Rule 3. This being observed, let him (if he is able) draw matter for meditation and prayer from his own needs and infirmities, from God's benefits, and from the changes and mortality of this life. He should chiefly meditate upon love, humility, meekness, peace of conscience, the glory of God's kingdom, His love, and those things contrary to it. But meditate especially on that which will be most available to you in the present moment.

Rule 4. If he cannot do this, let him first read part of Psalm 119, some of the epistles from the apostles, some of Christ's sermons (e.g., John 14–18), some part of this direction, or some of the meditations which follow, or any other good matter fit for this purpose, that he may season and well affect his mind. Let him do this so that he may learn how to perform this duty and quicken up himself to it often and regularly, once he knows how to do so.

If he cannot read, he must seek more help from others. And lacking help, he will move forward slowly in the right use of meditation and in any other part of sound godliness and Christianity. For we cannot be ignorant of this: the old and subtle sower sets his snares and nets so thick in our way, that we have no device for escape, except meditation and prayer by which we mount up high above them and fly over them. Those who cannot read will for the most part find this more difficult.

The Cost of Neglecting Meditation

Men lose a great part of their sweet and blessed life here, seeing they will not use meditation. Many even of God's servants through their corrupt nature loathe this heavenly manna of daily musing on the things which concern their peace. Their teeth are set on edge with the deceitful pleasures of worldly men, who know no better. For this reason alone they fail to enjoy a tenth of the privileges and liberties God has provided for them in their pilgrimage. And nothing could be less tolerable in the sight of almighty God than to be only seldom, coldly, and by fits occupied in meditation. For God has given us His Scriptures, which reveal His mind and teach us how to commune with Him. He has given them for our benefit and has charged us to ponder them in our hearts, to keep them in our minds, making them the matter of our meditation, delight, talk, and practice. It is wrong for Christians of good hope to treat God as if He were only trifling with us in this, or as though He were offering great injury to us in moving us to meditation.

Though I cannot say that these things (which should season all their thoughts) are never in their thoughts (though I might say this of many lying Protestants who shun and flee all consideration of heavenly things, lest they become troubled by them), yet it is too manifest that they do not favor God's presence and company when they shun it by being strangers to meditation, by which they could have fellowship with Him.

To remedy this trifling away the time when we seek to privately meditate and pray and to become better fit to perform this duty rather than be carried away with wandering thoughts, we must remove that which hinders us. We must tie up our loose hearts throughout the day from their deadly habit of wandering after vain and deceitful thoughts, dreams, and delights. We must weigh how little worth this is to have our thoughts attached to transitory things with delight (much less filthy and evil things). We must rather bring our thoughts to be taken up in heavenly things. We are called to this; and until we learn to do it, however weighty our other dealings may be, yet until we count this the best way to keeping peace with God and avoid offending Him we find it hard to bring ourselves to meditate and pray with cheerfulness and fruit.

CHAPTER 7

The Armor of the Christian

The third private help is the Christian's armor, which was next mentioned among the rest. Since the use and benefit of the armor is not as clearly understood, it requires fuller explanation than most of the other helps. In His mercy, God has appointed the armor to furnish the Christian soldier against all his spiritual enemies in all his warfare. And by help of the armor and the other means mentioned in this treatise, God enables the Christian to be rightly directed always, to keep a good course in his life, and to resist the strong and subtle assaults of the devil, that he be neither led nor overcome by them nor by the manifold bad passions and evil desires of his own heart, which otherwise will draw him continually after them. But before proceeding further, I will set down in general the points worthy to be learned and practiced in and about this armor. In this way, the reader will better see how to use it rightly. First, I will show what this armor is and explain its main parts. Secondly, I will show that the Christian life cannot stand without it. Unless the Christian is armed as God has taught and appointed, he cannot practice the Christian life. Thirdly, I will show how we get the armor and how to put it on. Fourthly, I will show (in the next chapter) the benefit of this armor and how by its help we may always practice godliness and be able to stand fast in our Christian course and resist in the time of danger. In this way, God will enable us to live Christianly, which is to have our citizenship in heaven with Him (Phil. 3:20), as He requires.

What the Christian Armor Is

The whole armor of the Christian is the spiritual equipment of the gifts and graces of the Holy Spirit by which God delivers His people from all power of the enemy and brings them to obey His will. I am not speaking here of those who are yet to be called, but of those who have already been effectually called. By the help of this armor, they not only cast down strongholds of temptation and overthrow imaginations and every high thing which exalts itself (in the thoughts of him that is tempted) against the knowledge of God, but also bring every evil thought in subjection to the obedience of Christ (2 Cor. 10:4–5). And this armor is that which is described in Ephesians 6:14–17, the parts whereof are these: the belt of truth (or sincerity); the breastplate of righteousness; the shoes of peace (or preparation to bear the cross); the shield of faith; the helmet of salvation (which in another place he calls "hope"); and the sword of the Spirit, which is the Word of God. This is the full furniture of a Christian by which the Lord has taught him to fight against the devil and his instruments, thereby to prevail in and through his captain and head, Christ Jesus.

Although there are other points of armor set down in other places of the Scripture, yet are they but aspects of this same armor expressed in other words. And there is no need for other armor, for he who is attired and armed with this will not be lacking provision or strength in time of need. But since not everyone readily sees how these graces may be considered as armor, I will describe each individual piece.

The Belt of Truth (Sincerity)

Sincerity or uprightness is that weapon or part of the spiritual armor and that fruit of the Spirit which should accompany the whole life (not a few actions) of the Christian, by which he is simple and without fraud and hypocrisy bearing away in him (2 Cor. 1:12), both toward God and his neighbor. We can discern this more clearly by considering the person in whom it is found—namely, an upright man, whom (in the description of Nathaniel) our Savior Christ calls a true Israelite in whom there "is no guile" (John 1:47). Although this virtue is a part of the Christian armor (Ps. 32:2; Matt. 5:8), it is rare. Not only do the best people see this, but even bad people complain about it; for in the words of Solomon, "Most men will proclaim every one his own goodness: but a faithful man who can find?" (Prov. 20:6). In other words, who will prove himself by word and example to truly be what he seems to be? The truth is that men are so infected with hollowness and hypocrisy and are so confirmed in it through habit, that until God changes the heart Jeremiah's words are as true of this as of other evils: "Can the Ethiopian change his skin, or the leopard his spots? then may ye also do good, that are accustomed to do evil" (Jer. 13:23).

This quality also consists in holding and keeping the truth—that is, keeping the sound knowledge of the Word in our judgment and the practice of it in a good conscience. For there are some who profess great friendship to the gospel who yet maintain strange opinions not according to the truth of it. For example, some say that the law should not in any wise be preached. Some say we should make no differences between men, even though the Scripture marks the difference between good and bad both in their life and in rewards (Ps. 1:1–3). Holding such opinions does not stand with sincerity. For sincerity requires all opinions to be measured and censured by the Word.

Now therefore, if sincerity and uprightness is to not only be free from double-heartedness and halting, but also to be ready to yield a frank assent and practice to the truth, and further, if this virtue is one part of the Christian armor, then he who is void of this lies open to great danger both by error in opinion and corruption in life. For he lacks that which will defend him. On the other hand, he who truly seeks to please God, his conscience bearing him record that he has some true measure of this sincerity, and who still labors to be simple and plain (though polite) in his words, actions, and meaning, he has this part of the armor. The beneficial use of this piece will hereafter appear. Thus, this is sincerity. But let me add this: if any purposes this in some things yet is not resolved to practice it in all things, this man is far from sincerity.

The Breastplate of Righteousness

Righteousness is that part of the armor and such a gift of the Spirit by which our hearts are bent to all manner of goodness and righteous dealing, approving of it as most excellent, fervently desiring it, and delighting in it (and that because it is good), and disliking and hating all wickedness and evil. And he who looks to be preserved in manifold temptations to sin and remains obedient throughout life to all kinds of duties toward both God and men needs no less than this firmness and constancy of a righteous heart and to be so thoroughly persuaded of the beauty and price of this one part of Christianity—namely, innocent and righteous dealing—that though infinite occasions will arise to diminish the credit of it, yet he may clothe himself with it as with a garment and wear it as an ornament, that he may show himself righteous in his actions and cause others to be in love with it also (Ps. 7:4; Prov. 28:1; Phil. 1:11). This virtue so shined in Joseph that many times when he might have without fear of revenge done evil to his brethren (who had given him great occasion), he would not (Gen. 45:3–4; 50:19). Neither would he listen to his whorish mistress, but refused it with detestation (though in so doing he brought himself into no small danger), saying, "How then can I do this great wickedness, and sin against God?" (39:9).

He that sees into this virtue and likes it so that he will be wary to commit no unrighteous thing against God nor man as far as his knowledge guides him, but settles himself to do that which is pleasing both in the sight of God and before men—he has this part of the armor and is fenced with the breastplate of righteousness. Such will say with Job, "If my adversary write a book against me, I will put it behind my back no matter who reads it, and glory in my accusations" (see Job 31:35–36). The beauty of this grace and virtue is such (as may appear in the examples of those who were found innocent when they were charged and accused, as in Ahimelech, Jonathan, and David toward Saul [1 Sam. 22:8–15; 24:1–7]) that if it could be seen with the eye, it would greatly provoke men to love it. And let all mark how fitly these two virtues, sincerity and righteousness (or innocence), go together.

The Shoes of Peace

To be prepared with the shoes of peace by the gospel is this: that just as those who are ready to take a long journey have put on shoes, so we, having received forgiveness of our sins and assurance of salvation through faith by the gospel (Rom. 5:1), are ready to deny ourselves and take up our cross and follow Christ throughout our pilgrimage. This piece of armor our merciful Father sees fitting for us, His weak children, seeing that we are so dismayed in hearing of future troubles (Luke 22:33–57), even though they were cheerful before. He therefore wants us to not faint or be discouraged, not even by trials, but to lift up our heads and be of good comfort, seeing that our trials are only temporary, while our peace is enduring and "passeth all understanding" (Phil. 4:7; cf. John 16:33). It is therefore able to keep our hearts comforted through hope, even in our tribulations. Our Savior foretold that the faithful would have this and graciously armed them against these trials.

Indeed, nothing else can keep us from deadly anxiety and bitter anguish at such times. For seeing that we are going to God through the most dangerous ranks of cruel enemies, as through a wilderness of robbers, this is our encouragement to courageously press on: that we know through the teaching of the gospel that we journey to

God, who is at peace with us and is therefore our guide and deliverer from them all. He therefore who has this peace by the gospel is armed with this part of Christian armor called the "shoes of preparation." As the soldier is armed with his brassy boots, so he is armed against all those difficult afflictions and sharp troubles which like pikes in the way would otherwise wound him, making him unable to stand in the battle. But he is armed because he thinks in his heart, "If God is for me, who can be against me?" (Rom. 8:31), and, "The LORD is my light and my salvation; whom shall I fear? the LORD is the strength of my life; of whom shall I be afraid?" (Ps. 27:1).

The Shield of Faith

To have the shield of faith is to build our persuasion on God's faithful promises that Christ Jesus is ours, and that God has given Him to us to obtain forgiveness of our sins and salvation by Him, yes and all other good things also necessary for this present life. As the apostle says, "He that spared not his own Son, but delivered him up for us all, how shall he not with him also freely give us all things?" (Rom. 8:32). He has this part of the armor who has embraced these precious promises and rests upon them, as certain and not doubtful, no more to be removed and unsettled, since (if it is well considered) there is no reason why he should be. Therefore, he will not be overcome by Satan's fearful temptations to strong unbelief, which like fiery darts are deadly to all who are not thus armed with a true and sound faith. Such a person may truly be said to put on the Lord Jesus, which is done only by faith.

The Helmet of Salvation (Hope)

This hope is a joyful longing (Rom. 12:12) and steadfast desire (as we may see in old father Simeon [Luke 2:30]) and looking for the accomplishment of all those temporal and eternal mercies God has promised and we are assured of by faith. For the Lord would have us know that He has made no one promise to us but He means to fulfill it, that we may see it and glorify Him for such lovingkindness of His toward us. Therefore, He would have us also in reverence to hope perfectly—that is, confidently and constantly to the end, as the apostle speaks—for such gracious gifts as He has given to us (1 Peter 1:13). While we are supported with this holy boldness, our hearts are so well satisfied and contented that we pass our days cheerfully and walk in our callings joyfully, serving God in them. Yes, we like our portions very well and enjoy our prosperity with much thankfulness.

And we do all this because we have hope from God for all good things which are needful for us. And we do hope for this not after the flesh or because we have whatever the heart can wish or the eye desire (for our God does not indulge us in this way), but because we have some measure of godliness with contentment and have learned to be persuaded that what God brings to pass is best for us. Therefore, we continue to hope that all things will fall out to us for the best (Rom. 8:28), because God has so promised. If it were not for this sweet hope, our lives would be most wearisome, unless we should suffer them to be merely devilish. And without this armor of hope, all other hope is vain and deceitful, like the rush which withers without moisture and the spider's web which is suddenly swept down.

The Sword of the Spirit

To have the last piece of armor, the Word of God, called the "sword of the Spirit," is to be well instructed in the sound and living knowledge of the Scriptures, to digest the same, and to season our understanding with it. We must do this so that we may know the will of God and have it in remembrance in the things that most concern us, that we may be led by it in all times and situations. As the prophet says, God's Word is a lamp to our feet and a light to our paths (Ps. 119:105). We must be so well instructed in the Word that we are not secretly deceived or carried away from our steadfastness in our Christian course (2 Peter 3:17) by either heresy in opinion or dangerous error in practice. Instead, we should draw forth this sword of the Spirit, saying, "Thus it is written in the Book of God," as our Savior said in similar situations. In stating and resting in the same, we will not be carried astray.

When such knowledge of good and evil, therefore, is lacking in us, or when we are neglectful rather than daily increasing in knowledge, then the adversary will pierce our souls with sore and perilous wounds. Even the most experienced and skillful Christian should not think he knows enough. Lest anyone should deceive himself about this, thinking that he has knowledge, I say this: if he is not counseled and guided by that which he understands, then he knows nothing yet "as he ought to know" (1 Cor. 8:2). For the fear of offending God is the beginning of wisdom, and he is most wise who keeps (that is, faithfully endeavors to keep) the command-ments of God (Prov. 1:7; 9:10). So spoke our Savior to His apostles: "If ye know these things, happy are ye if ye do them" (John 13:17). Therefore, this knowledge and the experience we learn by it is that part of Christian armor called "the sword of the Spirit." Who cannot see what a singular and necessary help it is to the practice of a godly life? For a man without the Word is as a blind man without a guide.

I have given the reader a taste of what the Chris-tian's armor is. By rightly considering the power and use of every piece of the armor, you may easily see that he who is furnished with the same will be able to do wonderful things in respect of him who goes to work by his own advice and power, or (which is the same thing) by mixing it with the Word of God. And yet most who profess the gospel do this: they will not altogether exclude God's commandments and refuse to be governed by them altogether; yet, for all that, they will not bind themselves to be ruled by them in all things—in one thing as well as in another. And therefore they jar and jangle in their life and talk in respect to their knowledge of their duty. If they would but seriously and carefully search into their ways at any time, they will see how their lives are harsh and unsavory, to both good and bad people, and to themselves also.

Having shown what the Christian armor is and having looked at its various parts, we have now covered the first point.

The Christian Life Cannot Stand without the Armor

The second point is that the Christian life cannot stand without this armor. He that is willing to live Christianly throughout his whole life must not be content to have the knowledge of the armor only in his head or in a book. He must digest this knowledge and make it his own. He must neither doubt the truth of the armor nor fail to put it on. He must be always ready to clothe and furnish his soul with the pieces of the armor. For as apparel clothes the body, so the armor covers his nakedness and shame, making him comely and well-favored in the sight of God. He must arm himself as the soldier arms himself with his breastplate, helmet, and sword, because God has appointed this armor to defend him from the craftiness of the devil, his deadly enemy, and from the deceitfulness of the most horrible sin.

All Other Helps Do Less Good without the Armor

He who considers this can be sure that all other good helps to godliness (such as prayer, reading, and godly conversation), though they are profitable in themselves, yet do Christians less good without the armor. Therefore, when the apostle taught the Ephesians to practice the specific duties of Christianity, he sends them to this armor to enable them to stand fast in their practice. Without this, he tells them, the devil with his subtle baits and delusions would draw them away from his exhortations, notwithstanding their desire to be obedient to the same.

The Devil Wounds Us If We Are Not Armed

The apostle thus writes, saying, "Take up the whole armor of God, that you may be able to withstand in the evil day"—that is, not only when the danger seems smaller, but in the hard time, when Satan bends all his force against you and proclaims (as it were) open war (Eph. 6:13). "And having done all"—that is, having resisted your enemy—"to stand" and keep yourselves continually armed against new assaults. Seeing the devil is a professed enemy of ours, an enemy who wounds us secretly when we are unaware and an enemy at hand to do us most harm when we least expect it, we know that if we are not prepared against such dangers, we will certainly be hurt. Who goes naked and unarmed into battle, where so many kinds of weapons are ready to take away his life? No, even when he has done all, it is little enough, though he is armed in every part.

Each Piece of Armor Is Necessary
The necessity of the whole armor in general will be better seen if we consider each specific piece. For who will venture to go barefooted among thorns? Or who will run among spikes without shoes? Even so, who will boldly go through the many storms and tribulations of this life, which in every place arise not to prick his feet but to pierce through his heart—who (I say) will go through these storms, but he who is well armed against them? Who, but he who is strongly prepared and settled to stay himself upon God by the peace and comfort which he draws from Christ's own words—namely, "In the world ye shall have tribulation: but be of good cheer; I have overcome the world" (John 16:33)?

And that which I say of this one piece, I may also say of all the other pieces which God has provided for the Christian, that there is no way for him to walk in safety through this world without the armor—every piece of it. Who can be free from despairing of God's mercy (for despair is a fiery and venomous dart), or from dreadful doubts and fears, or from presumption, vain hope, and self-deception (all of which are deadly and dangerous), unless he has the shield of faith? Only then is he certain of eternal salvation and of God's favor to guard him in this life. Though such a person has no other cause for unhappiness, yet without this it is enough to make all his pleasures tasteless.

Besides, what is his life, even at its best, when he has no trust in God's many promises? Though these things are not seen with the eye and little considered by most of the world, yet Scripture concludes that there is no peace to any such (Isa. 48:22). The devil, rather, like a roaring lion (1 Peter 5:8), has his paw upon their throat, ready in every hour to take away their souls, though this is neither known nor felt. But if they were shielded by this faith in all their need, it would not be so with them; for thereby they would resist him, and he would flee from them (James 4:7).

Again, to show how impossible it is to be in safety without the other parts of the Christian armor, how can anyone walk among neighbors in innocence and blamelessness, without having put on the breastplate of righteousness and armed himself with the purpose to do wrong to no one (and not only this, but to also avoid all iniquity and evil which might offend anyone or wound his own soul)? How many ways will he be led into sin against God and his neighbor? I am not speaking of an unbeliever, who can do nothing but sin, but of a Christian, who has a heart that hates sin. Yet, even he will be disfigured with many blemishes, if he does not purpose afresh in his heart to stand against all unrighteousness and all aspects of unholiness. He will disgrace himself and his holy profession by his many unlawful actions. But if innocence is in his heart and in his hands, he will live without blame and rebuke among men.

Therefore, Paul teaches the Corinthians to be clothed with the parts of the Christian armor, such as purity and uprightness, with knowledge of God's Word, and with patience and longsuffering. Paul commends to them by his own example "the armor of righteousness, on the right hand and on the left"—that is, in both prosperity and adversity. This he does so that they will give no occasion of offense in anything, but will in all things approve themselves as servants of God (2 Cor. 6:3–8).

The same may be said of the other parts of the Christian armor that I have said of the shoes of peace, of the shield of faith, and of the breastplate of righteousness. For if there be not some clear and sound knowledge of the Word of God (which as a sword may cut the bands of sin asunder like a cord), how will a Christian be able to discern the deceitfulness of sin, rather than be led and taken by it as with bait in a trap? If he has not learned well the Word and digested it in the depth of his heart, how can he avoid being led into many errors and going without the sweet life which is found in Christianity, even though he may desire to do well? And if he is not girded and adorned with sincerity, and all other good gifts of God in him bound together by sincerity, in which he holds them in truth and indeed delights in them, how will he not be infected with hollowness and hypocrisy, no matter what show of holiness appears in him?

To conclude, what can there be in his daily life but fainting, discomfort, and many discouragements, while he is weaned from the foolish, vain delights of this world, yet sees not the pleasures of heaven with mortal eyes? What else can there be for him, if the hope of salvation is not his helmet to keep life in his soul? And with this hope of salvation, which cannot deceive him, a cheerful hope of also safely passing the course of these conflicting days under the wings of God's protection? As for other hope, who does not know that any other hope of earthly peace or long life is like a broken tooth or sliding foot? But by this hope, tediousness is removed and cheerfulness to wait contentedly in this pilgrimage for a full deliverance is obtained. Therefore, it is true that the Christian life without the armor of God cannot be continued.

Every piece of Christian armor is needful throughout our lives. Even those who have been born anew to a living hope through God's grace and the preaching of the gospel need the armor. For they will not prosper, thrive, or grow into maturity in Christ, nor be delivered from the hindrances of the world, unless they are strongly armed, just as God has taught us to be.

God's Children Have No Strength against Sin at
Any Time, but by Means of the Armor

This is so truly verified in all God's children that even those who are not the most forward, yet if they have any strength against evil at any time, they have it from God by the means of the armor. If they were not always armed, they would make as great breaches and fall as dangerously one day as well as another. On the other hand, if they were thoroughly acquainted with this armor, they should make their worst and most uncomfortable day in the week equal to their best and happiest in passing their time in heavenly ways and in sweet comfort. And when they lack this armor (because of either being unknown or unused), they are vexed with infinite irksomeness, heaviness, distraction, sluggishness, doubting, and fear. Their hearts are occupied by other similar deadly poisons, such as frivolous rejoicing in a fleshly manner, vain hope, imaginary dreams of peace and safety where none is. Lacking the armor, their lives before others fail to show forth light and good example in one thing as well as in another. Rather, they harbor many evil qualities, insomuch that few are encouraged by them to become better, nor to suspect anything is amiss in themselves. Instead, they are hardened to continue in their ways.

And if this is so with those who have some good and sound beginnings in Christianity, let no one marvel that those utterly destitute of faith and of other parts of the Christian armor are so far from living a good life, for they renounce this arming of themselves, which I have proved a Christian life cannot be without.

How the Christian Armor Should Be Put On

By what we have seen of the armor up to this point, we have a better understanding of what it is, what the pieces of the armor are, and how the Christian life cannot stand without it. Now we proceed to the third point—namely, how to put the armor on. This will help us better understand how to benefit from the armor which God has provided for us.

Every Newborn Christian Has All the Parts of the Armor in Some Measure

The first thing to note is that every believer in and by his first conversion to God is made a partaker of all things pertaining to life and godliness (2 Peter 1:3). Therefore, the believer is not destitute of any grace that belongs to the true Christian. As a newborn child possesses all the parts and faculties of soul and body, yet is weak in them all, so it is with the newborn Christian. He has all necessary graces, though they are weak. And among these graces, these that are compared to the armor are principal.

Since this is true, when commanded to have this grace and the parts of the armor in readiness, the faithful Christian does not need to wonder whether he will have the armor or doubt how to come by it, for he already has it. As Christ our Savior said, "The kingdom

of God"—that is, God's glorious reign in the elect—
"cometh not with observation: neither shall they say,
Lo here! or, lo there! for, behold, the kingdom of God
is within you" (Luke 17:20–21). Therefore, this armor
which God has appointed to defend His militant church
from infernal slavery is not to be seen or gazed upon
with the eye. Rather, it is in the faithful and possesses
their souls, even now when many will (perhaps) ask how
they will come by it or where it is to be had. For if anyone should in ignorance imagine that he does not have
the armor after believing, how can he not be troubled
concerning how to get it or put it on, when he considers
the apostle's charge (Eph. 6:13–14; Col. 3:12, 14)?

Let us know, therefore, that we are not always to be
seeking this armor. This is unnecessary, especially when
we should be using it. For the Lord, knowing our needs,
has already provided each one of His children with the
armor to guard them from the infinite dangers of the
world. Each one of them has some measure of true faith
and hope, even if they are weak in them. Each one hates
iniquity and is ready to do righteousness, according to
his skill. The feeblest Christian has an upright heart and
some measure of spiritual wisdom with which to discern
good from evil (while a man of greater knowledge who is
not enlightened with the Spirit of regeneration cannot
have this), though some Christians have more than others. The same is true of the other graces.

To Put the Armor on Is to Have the Feeling and Use of It

So why does the apostle command us to put it on, if we already have it? His concern is that Christians not be like men in times of peace, who have bodily armor stored away, rusted, and utterly unfit for use. We should rather be like soldiers who put on their armor for battle and keep it on as long as the battle continues. Thus, he commands us not to let the pieces of this armor be so unused by us, that we have no feeling of it and therefore no benefit by it. Instead, we should be sure to continually have it on and ready for use. We should lay down in it and arise with it, wearing it throughout the day, everywhere we go.

This is what he means when he says, "Take unto you the whole armour" (Eph. 6:13), and in another place, "Put on therefore, as the elect of God, holy and beloved, bowels of mercies, kindness, humbleness of mind, meekness, longsuffering" (Col. 3:12). In other words, bind them to you and wear them, that, like your apparel, they may warm your souls and make you seemly. For our battle lasts all our lives, and our enemies are deadly, and all our strength is in the armor. Who therefore cannot now see that a Christian can never be safe without this armor? If this seems too difficult to anyone, they should know themselves to be those who lack the skill to put on the armor, and who are ignorant concerning its use and power. They have not learned well the will of God about the necessity and benefit of it. And therefore, though they may belong to the Lord, there is no doubt that the devil holds them in strong chains of darkness, ignorance, slavery, and bondage. God for His part has shown them the way out, if they but see it and be persuaded that it applies to them.

Through men's lack of skill in rightly using the armor and their lack of acquaintance with all its parts, the lives of God's dear servants are blemished, lacking honor among men. Among themselves, they are idle, unprofitable, and very uncheerful. Therefore, seeing that God has given them all needful helps for their defense from this present evil world, subjection to Satan, and their own damnable lusts, and seeing also that He has taught them to know their liberty and privilege and to have the daily help and benefit of their armor, for strengthening them in all good duties, I know of nothing which should trouble them any longer, no, not even the weakest, except this one thing: How do they put the armor on?

To Put the Armor on, We Must Watch and Pray

Now to have the feeling of every part of this armor—faith against distrust at any time, hope against fainting, uprightness against hypocrisy, knowledge against the deceitfulness of sin, righteousness against all kinds of iniquity, and the preparation of the gospel of peace against crosses—to have this armor ready to keep us and conduct us safely throughout our life in our practice of Christianity, this is to be done: we must watch continually and pray with heart (Matt. 26:41). This we must do often. The apostle also prescribed this when after exhorting the Ephesians to put on the whole armor he said to pray "always with all prayer and supplication in the Spirit, and watching thereunto with all perseverance" (6:18).

God wants us to be persuaded that we can possess and put on this whole armor and therefore to pray to Him for it. But these prayers must be made without doubting and wavering (James 1:6), for without this manner of praying we cannot look to receive anything. Seeing we are so prone to doubt, it has pleased our good God to give us a most sure word of promise. He promises to give us all things that we need. And if we believe God can be trusted, we may look for these things without fear or wavering.

The one who earnestly desires this as something which he cannot be without, seeing that he asks according to God's will for that which God commands, he will obtain that which he desires (1 John 5:16). He will ask and receive (Matt. 7:7). For if Hagar was heard, though she knew not how, when she prayed in her distress, and since our Savior told the Samaritan woman that if she had asked, He would have given her living water (John 4:10), then can it be doubted that God's dear servants will be denied their requests? If a natural father (who does not always know what is best and is not always as kind as he should be) will give his child what is needed, will we question the willingness of our heavenly Father—especially concerning a gift that He has bidden us to both ask for and receive, and such a gift as is necessary for honoring and serving Him rightly?

I speak this to strengthen and encourage you to pray both often and earnestly for this gift, that you may know that by this means you will put on the holy armor of God, especially when you watch and receive strength by prayers to do so.

And if this is not obtained by those who yet pray for it, it is because they pray faintly and coldly, or slackly and negligently (unless God is trying them, as sometimes He does even when they pray earnestly). For otherwise, this is the way to put on the whole armor of God.

Use Holy Meditation with Prayer

When we have been taught about the armor, prayer and holy meditation should be used upon each piece, until we know how to benefit from it. Until the meaning of the armor is more familiar to use, we should discuss the armor with those who have more knowledge and experience in it. In this way, those things that are difficult to understand and practice will be made easy. I say this for the benefit of the weak, since everything is harder for them, even if it is plainly explained to them. Either read what I have written for your sake, or read any sound treatise concerning it. Stir yourself up and persuade yourself of this: that you walk naked unless you are clothed with the armor. Without the armor, you are like an unarmed man fighting with many strong and well-armed enemies.

You have put the armor on when by reading, hearing, and godly conversation you see how your armor helps you to rightly frame your heart and life; and when you have meditated on the different pieces of it as I have prescribed and have duly weighed and mused upon the same to affect and season your heart with it; and when by confident prayer you have sought God to strengthen you with each piece of the armor. This is how you must put it on. When you know each piece and the purpose it serves and are willing to walk in this spiritual attire, you will be kept safe (as they say) from wind and weather— that is, from the world and the devil.

For then, having this grace of believing, hoping, living in righteousness and uprightness, you will bring forth the fruit of it, as you have occasion, throughout the day. You will give credit to God's promises in all seasons—hope, in one time as well as another, and uprightness (living without fraud), in one thing as well as another. But remember that even at your best you are still subject to infirmities. Lastly, this will enable you to perform your duties to both God and man—one man as well as another. In so doing, you will show forth the fruit of the armor of righteousness. The same can be said of the other pieces.

The Armor Being Put on Must Be Kept On

Along with all we have said, let it also be known that just as the armor must be put on in the way we have explained, so it must also be kept on. For example, in order to retain or recover one piece of this armor, such as peace or rejoicing (which we must never be without), this requires continual prayer. For after telling us to rejoice always, Paul also tells us to pray continually (1 Thess. 5:16–17; cf. Phil. 4:4, 6). He says that by putting on the whole armor we will be able to stand in the evil day (Eph. 6:13). In like manner, Peter says that if we give all diligence to joining our faith with virtue, knowledge, patience, and so on (and who does not know that this is chiefly done by watching and prayer?), we will never fall (2 Peter 1:5–11). That is, we will not fall dangerously to any great harm. By this Peter shows that he agrees with Paul, that for furnishing ourselves with the graces of the Spirit (which are the several pieces of the armor), we must use continual care and diligence, with watchfulness and prayer. This is the only way to put and keep the armor on.

The Weakest As Well As the Strongest Christian Must Wear the Armor

Let the reader here remember and consider who the Lord speaks to when He commands them to put the armor on, having it ready against all spiritual craftiness. For the one who has not yet fully resolved to be a Christian and lead a godly life is utterly unfit for this armor, having neither mind nor desire for it; neither can he possibly put it on. On the other hand, God commands both the strong Christian and the newborn babe, the weakest youngling in God's family who has the smallest ability to resist and withstand sin, to take up this armor and put it on. It is the equipment God has appointed to save him from danger, even the greatest danger that can be raised against him. Who therefore can keep him from this armor? For it keeps his soul and his life. What therefore should make him such a slave to fear and full of distrustful fantasies and discouragements, so that he casts away his weapons and offers himself into the lion's mouth? Therefore, every Christian must boldly and reverently take up the armor (for no one who lacks it is safe), especially when he sees who encourages him— namely, God all-sufficient, who is able to strengthen him. This should embolden him to keep his crown and honor (Rev. 3:11), even this whole armor, which is more precious to him than life itself. He should allow nothing or no one to take it from him.

I say this for their sakes who desire to apply the things I exhort, but whose understanding is weak concerning the nature of this armor and how it is used to make a Christian strong against sin and Satan, much less do they receive benefit from it (to their knowledge). And yet, they are not without the armor. I write this so they will see that their situation is better than they have thought, that God has provided for them far better than they were persuaded. Therefore, let them no longer be ignorant of it, neither let them be slothful in putting and keeping the armor on.

If they grow cold, let them urge themselves to use the means already mentioned by which the armor is put on. If the means grow tasteless to them, as ordinary prayer and watchfulness easily do, and if their hearts are discouraged or set in evil delights, let them drive out the devil with fasting and prayers, giving no rest to their eyes or ease to their hearts until they have recovered their first love and strength, which they once had by this armor.

Let them persuade themselves that if they do not wake up, fearful danger is not far away. It will come speedily. For though a weak Christian may at first feel the armor to be strange and wearisome (much like a new soldier with his bodily armor) and may wish to be unburdened of it, yet when he considers that God has given him this armor to benefit him, he will be admonished to think and act otherwise.

CHAPTER 8

The Benefit of This Armor

Now we come to the fourth point concerning the doctrine of the armor.

The Benefit of This Armor

He who learns to put on this armor and go clothed in it throughout the day will find that everything God has spoken, as I have here written, is true. For the devil flees the one who resists him and has fastened to his soul these pieces of armor. Therefore, the depth and subtlety of hell will not prevail against him. This is the fruit and use of the armor for those who take delight in being watchful to be so clothed, as no one should doubt. For as Paul writes to the Corinthians, "(For the weapons of our warfare are not carnal, but mighty through God to the pulling down of strong holds;) casting down imaginations, and every high thing that exalteth itself against the knowledge of God, and bringing into captivity every thought to the obedience of Christ" (2 Cor. 10:4–5).

Therefore, whether the devil and his instruments assault by craft and deceit or by force and might, the Christian who is armed as has been said and who is furnished with this strength will mightily prevail against them and preserve himself.

The Benefit of Faith

Such is the power of this armor that Scripture gives wonderful commendation to even one piece of it, ascribing to faith alone the victory that has overcome the world and its deceits (1 John 5:4). Peter, likewise, tells us to resist the devil, being "stedfast in the faith" (1 Peter 5:9). And our Savior says, "All things are possible to him that believeth" (Mark 9:23). For all things which we desire are not only possible but easy, since we have a promise from God upon which we firmly rest.

The Benefit of Uprightness

And just as the benefit of this one piece of our armor— namely, faith—is singularly great and its power mighty, so may it be said of the rest. Consider, for example, a pure heart. For this piece is able to carry us through strong temptations, so that we will deal not deceitfully, as men of the world do, but with integrity. An upright heart also keeps us joyful, as the apostle says, while those who lack it must hold down their heads. To say no more, a pure heart makes our condition happy. This is according to that which is written, "Blessed are the pure in heart" (Matt. 5:8).

Now therefore, if just one part of this heavenly attire is so helpful and of such great use, what can we say of the whole armor? Indeed, to be clothed with the complete armor of a Christian gives us safety in our walk against the subtleties of the devil, the allurements of the world, and the deceitfulness of sin. In this way, a Christian may go through many dangerous attempts unwounded. Yes, he can even enjoy sweet communion with God throughout the day, though he is not to flatter himself or live in dangerous presumption.

The Benefit of Righteousness and Preparation for the Cross

He must also be resolved to put on, and clothe himself, with righteousness and preparation for the cross by the defense and shelter of the doctrine of the gospel during his warfare in this life. Preparation for the cross will bring to him meekness, patience, and longsuffering with joy (when God afflicts him), while righteousness will lead him to love his enemies and be innocent toward all (for these are branches of righteousness) and keep him from being led after contrary evils. For all these duties and many more, which are fruits of the tree of righteousness, planted and watered by God in the fruitful ground of his heart—all these, I say, the armed believer will bring forth in abundance.

The Benefit of the Word of God

Likewise, the one who has set himself to seek wisdom as gold and lay up understanding as treasure (cf. Prov. 2:4–6) will be taught the good and perfect way, while others will always reel and fall. Yes, when others forever walk and wander in byways (even though they seek the way), the believer thus armed will clearly see the king's highway before him. He will know and be guided by the will of God, and therefore his steps will be pleasant as he walks in the plain and known way, rather than the way which is rough and uncertain.

I could show the same fruit from the rest of the pieces, but I have done so already and do not want to grow tedious. If we therefore love to go armed in these holy weapons with the measure of knowledge God has taught us; and if we daily enjoy new growth, armed with the righteousness and godliness we can reach and attain; and if we are upheld in that hope God has put within us and are strengthened with faith in all His promises, so that we are by the gospel kept in our afflictions with peaceful and quiet hearts, as God has encouraged us— then we will be able to live with good consciences in all the situations and places to which God leads us. We will not be changed by circumstances, seeing that God has strengthened us until we see an end of all difficulties and uncertainties.

We Should Not Think Ourselves Ready in the Morning until Armed

All who consider these things should heed this needful advice: to not think themselves ready for the day until they have put on the Lord Jesus (Rom. 13:14) with His wisdom, righteousness, sanctification, and redemption (1 Cor. 1:30). We do this when by faith we count Him as ours. In this way we lack nothing, for Christ can help us in all things. When we are defended against the evils of the day by this help, we have acquitted ourselves. We should do this every day, for this is the reason God has given us this mighty armor.

If you can be resolutely persuaded to arm yourself in this way throughout the warfare of your life, I am sure that you will be led into the only safe, pleasant, profitable, beautiful, and happy way. In a short time, you will say it yourself. For through experience you will find that your days far exceed your former days (before understanding this help) in beauty. For the longer you abide in this practice, the better you will find it and the more you will come to love it.

It does not matter how ignorant you are, if you have enough knowledge to see that this is the best of all other ways. And it does not matter how weak you are, if you are strong enough to be persuaded to walk in it and see your need for what I have said, once God inclines your heart to leave other ways of which He disapproves and settles you in this way which He has commended.

The Longer a Man Uses This Armor, the
More He Will Love It

When you see that you are acquainted with this armor and how it helps you to live in innocence and Christlikeness, then consider what you have and how rich it makes you, and what great privileges the Lord has thereby given you. When you reap its fruit, this will be no grief to you (1 Sam. 25:31). Be glad and thankful for the armor, more than if you had found great treasure. Weigh the great protection you have by the armor against the devil, the safe conduct from falls, the fears and doubts you are delivered from, the mists of ignorance that are plucked from your heart. Consider how the scales have been taken from your eyes. Consider the strength you now find against your strongest enemies and how easily you may turn back into the way when you have slipped in weakness. More than this, consider the peace you have in your conscience and rest for your soul, when you see (more clearly than before you were thus armed) not only that there is no condemnation for you (Rom. 8:1), but also how God fights for you and makes you fit to resist the deceitfulness of strong temptations, though before you were so weak and impotent in resisting them.

Though you are not free from all temporal afflictions, yet you can never sufficiently esteem the value of this blessed condition. You will often think it is too good to last, until you remember that there is no shadow of turning with God (James 1:17). You will often wonder at God's generosity toward you, that you should have such sweet communion with Him, and such confidence and boldness before Him in all your difficulties, whereas most of the world is subject to the most dreadful fear of His vengeance, as often as God shows them their danger. When you feel these things and the value of being fenced in from the daily vexations with which most men are troubled, then you will not doubt whether you are willing to keep this armor on, for you will see that you cannot consider yourself well without it.

Why Some Believers Are Held Back from This Blessing
But who finds this liberty in his life? Or what manner of arming can keep someone in safety from the many evils most men complain of daily? In answer, I know many such people (praise God) who with peace of conscience enjoy this liberty and safety. And I am sure there are many more whom I do not know. Yet I am persuaded that thousands of God's dear servants are held back from this blessing through the malice of our enemy. Through his subtlety they are held back by ignorance of this liberty (for they do not think God honors His servants with such privileges while they live here on earth and therefore count it presumption to expect it). Others know these things but favor themselves in their present wants and infirmities and exercise little violence against themselves. Therefore, they are held back from enjoying this comfort and blessedness in their lives.

Know this: the main reason why Christians are not further acquainted with this armed life and its blessed fruits is because they allow their hearts to take their fill of the world's delights, they give little effort in musing upon this heavenly state, and they offer weak prayers for it. Many others, though they are not utterly without faith, do not attain this state because they do not understand God's will for them to live according to a certain direction throughout their lives and be armed to this end. They serve God in a general manner, but without any great watchfulness over their particular actions.

But if they consider this burdensome, they must be content to sometimes be brought to shame for their doings and sometimes to terror and torment of conscience for their slippery walking and small regard for honoring God in one duty as well as another. For these are the properties of sin and cannot be separated from it. Though they do not fear such things, yet sooner or later they will come. Those who do not settle themselves soundly in the Christian life should expect much shame and sorrow which some of God's other servants will not have. And if this is the case with them, what is the state of the hypocrites and profane?

Without Much Striving, We Do Not Overcome
Some may be troubled by what I have said about the power and use of the armor and think that I have written untruth, since I have not spoken much about the strong

and raging enemies we fight against and how many good servants of God have been subdued by these enemies in temptations. Some might say I have not written of the conflicts and combats they have with the allurements of sin, as if they resisted and overcame them with ease and without any great striving. To answer, my full treatment of conflicts belongs to another treatise, where I discuss hindrances, whereas here I speak only of the armor.[1] Yet no one should understand me to think that our sins and lusts are easily overcome, for they are furious and raging. Satan's suggestions are skillfully shaped to deceive us and have a mighty force to allure us, and these must be resisted. As every observant reader may gather, I count it the hardest and most difficult of all things to subdue and conquer them. That is why I show such necessity of being continually armed against them. Therefore, we must strive courageously and stand upon our watch, for we cannot be crowned unless we strive lawfully (2 Tim. 2:5)—that is, steadfastly.

Even When Defeated, We Are Not as Miserable as Those Who Do Not Fight

We may be (and often are) defeated, as if hope of victory and of prevailing against our enemies was past. This is true even though we have the armor, because we are yet unskillful or faint and are fearful in using it. Yet in our

---

1. This was the subject of treatise 5.

weakest state, we are not forsaken by God. Though we are distressed and sorrowful for a time, we are not swallowed up. Though we are in discomfort, we are not in despair (2 Cor. 4:8). When we are at the lowest ebb, so that we yield to some temptation and are overcome by it, even then we are not as miserable as those who do not strive at all. We are left to ourselves for a while, so that we will see our weakness and afterward gain more strength, catch our breath (as it were), take better hold, and resist more valiantly, especially when we were overcome through our own faults. And yet, when it is so with us, who can deny that the reason it happened was because we were not better armed? For we were either unskillful or slothful in using the armor. I therefore repeat what I said before, that whatever our temptations and assaults are, we prevail and rejoice by the help of the armor Christ our Captain has taught us to keep on. In contrast, if we are naked and unarmed in battle, we will have sorrow. But we have good cause to be upheld and to cheerfully battle against all kinds of enemies, for we, like Joshua, have the promise of victory, for the weapons of our warfare are mighty.

Two Further Objections Answered

I have thus shown how the third help—namely, the Christian armor—advances us in a godly life. Now I will answer two objections. Some people will doubt that their failure in putting and keeping on this Christian armor causes their condition to lack honor and comfort. Others think that though the armor is fitting for strong Christians, weak ones should not be troubled with seeking for it but may content themselves to serve God without it, as they can. For, they reason, we discourage the weak when we lay such strong loads and burdens upon them.

No Safety without the Armor

In answer to the first objection, why should any think they can be good Christians without the armor, when they must see that if they walk nakedly, they cannot walk in safety? I do not deny that a Christian who fears and believes in God can be ignorant of this armor. But let them not say that they may serve God well enough without it. For what substance of godliness is in such a life, seeing it is found idle and unprofitable? What godliness is there in a wandering course of life? They should not rest in any condition without help of the armor. It is easily seen, then, how those who consider the force and use of the armor gain strength to live godly lives. It is therefore ignorant to say we may serve God as we should, even though we have no acquaintance with the armor.

The Armor Is a Help, Not a Burden

The second objection is that the armor is too heavy a burden for weak Christians. But this objection is as unsavory as the first. For those who are newborn Christians, the weakest and feeblest in God's family, are no sooner delivered from the slavery of Satan and fear of damnation, but if they could speak would first ask how to always abide in the estate of salvation in which they now find themselves. They desire to never forget God's kindness but feel and enjoy it every hour of every day. They want to honor Him for it, to testify their thankfulness, and to always please Him in all kinds of conditions, and for this cause to know His will. And these are the purposes the armor serves. Even the weakest Christian has this desire, just as infants cry for nourishment. No one needs to fear that we burden them by offering to them the very things they most desire. As it is the nature of a seed to sprout out of the ground in hope of harvest, even though it is held back by storms and cold, so the young Christian desires to be helped forward and clothed in these graces, as he can reach them. And what is this but the desire to be well armed, so that he may daily honor and obey God and keep his soul in safety? It is true that he is not settled in this to his satisfaction. But who marvels at this? Does not the young child, like the tender plant, have its season to grow? And when they sprout and flourish, will not all say that they prosper, though they have their winters as well as their summers? So it is with the beloved, though weak, Christians. These children of God, though they have many discouragements and hindrances (which are like the stormy cold is to young plants) and many sore doubts, fears, discomforts, and hindrances to growth from the devil and their own strong corruptions, yet, being rooted in good ground and well watered and weathered, they grow up and prosper as the Lord's plants.

A Caution to Those Who Do Not Desire the Armor
Perhaps there are some people who having seen zealous, godly Christians have been pricked in conscience for their sin. They seem to receive comfort from and be earnest lovers of the Word. They even seem to bring religion to others. But if they are not armed against sin, they (much less newborn babes in Christ) are fit to be urged with it. To these I say that if they do not use the armor, it does not matter what effects the ministry has had, nor how they have been affected by hearing the word, nor their zeal in professing it. It has already been proved that the weakest, if they are the Lord's, desire the armor. Therefore, those who do not, though they may think themselves good enough without it, may question whether they are truly the Lord's, even though there may be more commendable things in them than others. This should not seem strange. For both in Scripture and experience many have shined as lights for a season and in show of zeal and godliness have been (both among the ministers and people) esteemed above most others, yet for all this have shamefully fallen from what seemed to be their first love. It is no marvel then that this urging of the Christian armor does not taste well to them, though it is savory to the newborn in God's household.

It is not fitting here to deal further with those who seem even more forward. Only let them consider that it is dangerous to have once been in likelihood of goodness and now not to be. In contrast, "The path of the just is as the shining light, that shineth more and more unto the perfect day" (Prov. 4:18).

Therefore, I conclude what I proposed to answer: that putting on the Christian armor is not too strong a meat for the youngest ones nourished up in God's house nor too great a burden to lay upon them, but will rather help them more fruitfully and cheerfully serve God.

CHAPTER 9

Spiritual Experience and Company in Family Exercises

I have showed how the previously mentioned three private helps—watchfulness, meditation, and the Christian armor—are singular means to help us advance in living godly lives. I now turn to the fourth private help, spiritual experience. My purpose is to show how experience is a means to confirm us in faith and obedience. This I will prove after I have explained what it is and how far it reaches.

What Spiritual Experience Is

Spiritual experience is related to the piece of armor called the sword of the Spirit—that is, the Word of God—for it concerns the knowledge we learn by proof or trial for our spiritual progress. There are two aspects to knowledge. There is the knowledge we get by rule and the knowledge we get by proof or trial. The letter of Scripture gives us knowledge by rule. By the application of Scripture, we learn by trial. Experience concerns this second aspect of knowledge.

Spiritual Experience Compared with Worldly

We can better understand what this experience is when we consider it in this way: compare it with experiential knowledge in any trade or science. There is a difference between bare, naked skill in a trade and experience in using the skill. So also in matters heavenly and spiritual. There is a difference between experiential knowledge and the bare knowledge that men have by rule or instruction only.

For example, perhaps someone is trained in an occupation and has knowledge and skill in his trade, but is unable to use it to the best advantage and greatest profit. Perhaps he does not know how, where, and when to buy and to sell, or how to position things so that he thrives and prospers rather than falling behind. He is ignorant of these things all for lack of experience, while he who has experience is able to do these things as God sees fit to bless.

So it is in spiritual things. For a man who has been plainly taught from the Word of God and catechized in the principal points of Christian religion is able by this help to confess his faith, give an account of the hope within him, and kindly answer questions put forth to him. But if he goes no further in bringing forth fruit toward God's kingdom, all this is but the knowledge of the letter. But the Christian who has experienced this knowledge so that it has been effectual to him and has assured him of his own salvation and has reformed and changed him, casting out the filthiness of heart and life which was in him before—he has received a different kind of blessing than the other and daily is likely to receive more.

This is what I mean by experience. For by this a Christian considers, observes, and applies the things which he hears. By duly regarding the past, he gains wisdom to guide him for the present and the future.

How Far Experience Reaches

Now to show how far experience reaches, we may understand that it makes us wise in all things which are profitable to godliness and eternal life, so that our life is little worth if we are not helped by this. For until we begin to mark how true every part of God's Word is, and how God daily executes in the world those things He says He will bring to pass, we neither reverence nor regard God's Word. Instead, we honor it only in speech and show. We do not fear to do wrong until we mark how God punishes the hollow-hearted and workers of iniquity. And in contrast, until we find how sweet and pleasant it is to be gathered under the Lord's wings and what a shelter and defense He is to His faithful servants, we make no reckoning of His service, but find it unsavory and unwelcome. But the experience of God's dealing toward us and the posture of ourselves toward Him in ways that bring the most rest to our souls brings the true fear of God. This is the only wisdom.

Remembrance of the past and God's work in it is one of the most powerful means, under God's blessing, for helping us make better progress in the Christian way. For when we can say, based on experience, that it always goes well with those who are upright in heart and innocent in their lives, this establishes us more constantly in the course of godliness. The same holds true when we consider of ourselves that we have seen good days and lived in comfort when we have walked after the same rule and have kept ourselves from the defilements of the world. When we have observed that God has punished presumption, ill conscience, rashness, and willful sinning, this experiential knowledge brings great wisdom in the choice of our ways. It causes us to take heed to ourselves, that it may go well with us. Our experience of the fruit of godliness is the best means for continuing in it.

For example, when in our troubles we have humbled ourselves before God, confessed our sins, and sought pardon in faith; when we have borne our trials with patience, in hope (though it seemed unlikely at the time) of seeing a good end to them; and when we have found and obtained this blessing, it is a clear demonstration to us that in similar troubles we will find the same blessing if we use the same means. This experience will not fail us, if those things we have attributed to God are agreeable to the Word which He has spoken. We find this often in David, the dear servant of God. He was both comforted in his affliction when he remembered the past, and he was constant in godliness, because he had marked how it always leads to a peaceful end (1 Sam. 17:34–37; Pss. 37:37; 77:10–11; 120:1).

And what marvel should this be to anyone who is trained up in the Lord's house? For we know that in trades and sciences beginnings are most difficult and most full of discouragements. So it is with Christians. They are most doubtful and full of weakness when first entering the Christian life. Yet who cannot remember that even then God worked lovingly and dealt with them tenderly, when their faith was yet so weak and young they could not easily discern it? But God kept many of them from sore falls. He held from many great afflictions and did not bring many of their sins to light at once, lest they should have been discouraged with how awful they were and how many there were. For God has promised to regard their weakness. Otherwise, they would have been driven to great adversity.

Why has the Lord done these things, if not for His children to observe them and learn experience by them for the times which will afterward come? And that they might safely and boldly promise to themselves greater proof of His assistance and fatherly kindness toward them? And why has He given a good end of their former chastisements when they penitently desired it? Even to this end: that their hope may be strengthened for the times that will come after. As the apostle speaks of himself and other godly people, God "delivered us from so great a death, and doth deliver: in whom we trust that he will yet deliver us" (2 Cor. 1:10). Why else has God preserved them from fearful falls when they earnestly desired it? Why has He made the way of godliness easier than they could have hoped for? The reason was to encourage them to look more confidently for the same grace and blessing in those times when they need proof of God's kindness and faithfulness to His promises, when they seek Him in the same manner as they once had. For the Lord's hand is not shortened that He cannot help (Isa. 59:1), but is near to them, as they are better acquainted with Him to believe it. Therefore, as men who have found a way to make a profit cannot be turned from it, so it is with these, when they by experience have found the sweetness of the Christian life.

It Is Woeful That Men Do Not Learn from Experience
But it is woeful that where so great benefit and gain might be reaped by such little effort—that is, by marking God's manner of dealing with His servants—that so few are brought to this wisdom and are persuaded to seek out the best and happiest way, and which is not difficult for those who gladly find it (Prov. 14:6). For the truth is that few people, when they have often hurt

because of their foolishness, set themselves to this work of gaining experience. Despite it all, they love to stay in their foolishness. (They are more foolish than children, who cannot be made to come near the water again after they have once been in danger of drowning.) And so they verify the words, "How long ye simple ones, will ye love simplicity?" (1:22). For this cause, many hearers are dead and cold practitioners—even many teachers, though they boldly utter what they have read, yet they are faint followers of what they teach. Or they conceal much of what they should deliver, because they do the opposite themselves. They see that, should they teach others, they would shun the reproach of the proverb: Physician, heal your own disease.

Seeing such a suitable occasion, I do not think it is out of season to add one more thing concerning this. I have thought much about this, having observed the course of men's lives and those also not of the worst sort. I well remember when I was a young man and first began to look after the life to come, I knew one who began to preach (I am not ashamed, thank God, to acknowledge that I loved such company thirty-eight years ago). The text he was to handle at a certain time gave him necessary occasion to reprove a sin, which he clearly saw himself to have often committed, though he had never much observed it until that time. He knew he should speak against it; but when he considered it, seeing such a blemish in himself, he was pricked in his conscience and deeply troubled that he must openly speak against a sin before his hearers of which he was guilty in the sight of God and of his own conscience. Being in supply to preach the next day, he broke off his study. He could not resolve to rebuke something in others when he was himself an offender in the same thing and so lay burdens on others when he himself seemed innocent. He humbled himself before God, confessed his sin, and professed the forsaking of it, craving forgiveness for it, before he dared proceed in the study for his sermon. After that, he was wary to always do this in his preaching—namely, to clear himself of that sin which he must condemn in others. Even then, I thought this to be a virtue in him. But since then I have noted how rare it is in men of his calling. Thus those who make it their consideration and wisdom to do as he did—namely, to make conscience of themselves before they urge others, and to mark what this blessed course of life is and how it is attained, so that they themselves cannot rest quiet without this— will be sure to find a singular help to godliness which they will never regret seeking after.

The Fifth Private Help: The Use of Company in Family Exercises

It follows in the next place how God has provided no less help for us in company than by ourselves alone. But because we have frequent use of it and many occasions to be in it, both in our own families and with others, it is possible for us to return from it worse than we went into it and to offend in it much. (For most companions make men more corrupt than they were before.) Therefore, the Lord has taught His people how to carry themselves in all their meetings with others in such a way as to not only shun the harm which is easily received, but also to gain much help and progress by it so as to go better forward in Christian duties. But, since this point is handled at large in the next treatise, I refer the reader there.[1]

---

1. Rogers gives further directions for both company and family exercises in chapters 15 and 19 of treatise 4. Rogers summarizes the aim believers should adopt in relationship with others: "The general rule to be observed in all company is that we fear danger, and are harmless in them and without offense, leaving no ill savor by example behind us. But more particularly, the mark we are to aim at in all our familiar company is this: that we should not rush unadvisedly into it as most men do, but determine beforehand to do good to others as we are able, and to help them forward unto eternal life by every good opportunity we can; or purpose to benefit from others, as occasion will be offered."

CHAPTER 10

Private Prayer and Its Parts

Having now explained the two first kinds of private helps, the third follows,[1] containing the helps which may be used by one's self alone, or with others also, such as prayer and reading. Prayer is a calling upon God according to His will and has these parts: thanksgiving, confession of sins, and request.

The First Part of Private Prayer: Thanksgiving

Thanksgiving is that part of prayer in which we are drawn to love and praise God and show the fruits of love and praise, because we have been comforted by some benefit which God has bestowed upon us in favor. In this description, we see three duties required of us in thanksgiving and three motives to draw us to perform

---

1. Rogers is referring to the threefold division of private helps as explained in his introduction: helps that are used by individuals alone, helps that are used in company with others, and helps that may be used either alone or with others.

them. I will first explain the motives and then proceed to the duties.

Motives for Thanksgiving

The first motive is knowledge and remembrance of some benefit received by us or promised to us. This may be seen in the thanksgivings of all God's servants—such as David, after he had received seasonable counsel from Abigail (1 Sam. 25:32), and in Abraham's servant, when God had blessed him in his journey to Aram (Gen. 24:27). The same may be said of the leper, when he saw that he was cleansed, after asking Christ for it (Luke 17:15). Where there is no knowledge and due consideration of some specific mercy, how can there be any true and heartfelt thanksgiving—even though there may be a declaration of thanksgiving in words for the sake of appearance, as in those who thank God for everything, though they consider nothing which moves them to give thanks?

The second motive is joy and gladness of heart for the benefit which we call to mind. This is evident in the psalm of those who returned out of captivity, saying, "When the LORD turned again the captivity of Zion, we were like them that dream. Then was our mouth filled with laughter, and our tongue with singing" (Ps. 126:1–2). And so, to apply this to ourselves, unless we find such sweetness and comfort in God's benefits either already received or promised and embraced by faith, there is no way for us to perform the duty of thanksgiving. This is confirmed in the common saying, that a work is not done well if it is not done cheerfully.

The third motive is a persuasion that the benefit for which we give thanks comes to us from God's fatherly love. This motive is most suited to produce the joy mentioned above, for God's fatherly love is a far greater reason for us to be glad than any benefit bestowed upon us in and of itself (116:5–16). For we would find little sweetness in such a benefit, if we feared that it was sent as a snare to entangle us or to heap hot coals upon our head and to make our condemnation more just, as when Christ gave a sop to Judas before he left to betray Him. The benefit would then be quenched with fear and an accusing conscience.

For example, what heartfelt joy or sound thanks could the Pharisee give (Luke 18:11)? Though he gave thanks with his tongue, yet his countenance showed the contrary because he did not have this persuasion of God's fatherly love. But, thank God, this is not the case with His beloved ones. For they, knowing that their most loving Father has given them the greatest gift, even Christ, how much more does He freely give them all things (Rom. 8:32)? These things are of less account, but both rejoice their hearts when they remember any of these His blessings and stir them up to a more heartfelt performance of this duty.

Duties of Thanksgiving

As these three motives must be found in us to move us to true thankfulness, so to make it effectual three duties are required: first, continuing in our love for God; secondly, a desire to set forth God's glory in words professing and confessing His goodness; and thirdly, further progress in obedience and walking worthy of His kindness.

The first duty is continuing in our love for God. For how can we not choose but to love and set our hearts upon Him, when we see the fruits of His favor on every side wherever we turn, for they are "new every morning" (Lam. 3:23)? As the prophet says, "I love the LORD, because he hath heard my voice and my supplications" (Ps. 116:1), and for His great and many mercies, which there he counts. But those whose love is set upon the gift or benefit itself, being little moved toward the giver and bestower of the gift, no matter how wide their mouths are open in giving thanks, they are far from rightly offering thanks to God.

The second duty is desire for God's glory. If we love the Lord, we will also be carried with a fervent desire for God to be known and believed on by others (2 Cor. 4:13), that they might come out of darkness. Neither can we satisfy ourselves in seeking to advance and magnify Him. As we may see in David, who being stirred up by the consideration of God's benefits had this affection in him and declared the same: "What shall I render unto the LORD for all His benefits toward me?" (Ps. 116:12)—as if he should say, "Oh that I knew and could satisfy myself in this!" Where this affection and desire exists, how can it be otherwise but there should be an expressing and acknowledging of this His goodness in every opportunity? The same person sets himself down to us for an example: "I will praise the LORD" and call upon Him with thanksgiving "in the congregation," in heart and tongue and with many kinds of well-tuned instruments (cf. 111:1, and many other places). And that which he does himself, he exhorts others to do as well— four times in one psalm, saying, "Oh that men would praise the LORD for his goodness, and for his wonderful works to the children of men!" (107:8, 15, 21, 31).

The third duty is further progress in obedience. Along with these two duties, we must join the third, that we faithfully endeavor to walk worthy of His kindness and to keep ourselves within holy limits, which is to do the will of our heavenly Father. When we do this, we rightly perform this duty of thanksgiving. But if this is missing from the rest, it makes them lame and maimed and odious to God, as the mortlings[2] and untimely firstborn of the beasts, which were offered to Him in sacrifice. Moses shows how reformation of our lives should also be joined to thanksgiving by setting down the danger of the contrary, saying: "And it shall

---

2. "Mortlings" refers to wool taken from dead sheep.

be, when the LORD thy God shall have brought thee into the land which he sware unto your fathers, to Abraham, to Isaac, and to Jacob, to give thee great and goodly cities, which thou buildest not, and houses full of all good things, which thou filledst not, wells digged, which thou diggedst not, vineyards and olive trees, which thou plantedst not; when thou shalt have eaten and be full; then beware lest thou forget the LORD, which brought thee forth out of the land of Egypt, from the house of bondage" (Deut. 6:10–12). The psalmist thus says, "What has thou to do to declare my statutes, or that thou shouldest take my covenant in thy mouth?" either in thanks, prayer, or speaking about it, "seeing thou hatest instruction, and castest my words behind thee" (Ps. 50:16–17).

These are the necessary three duties required in true thankfulness. I have therefore explained what thanksgiving is and what properties are required in it, that it may rightly be performed to God.

How Thanksgiving Is a Help to Godliness
Now then, if this duty be thus performed of us in adversity as in prosperity—for so God will have those who worship Him righty do (Job 27:10), and alone by ourselves as well as in company with others, so that we are free from hypocrisy in offering it—must it not then (along with the others) be a singular help to godliness? When we think upon God's great lovingkindness

toward us many times from day to day (1 Thess. 5:18) and find sweetness in His benefits and are persuaded that we have them in God's favor; and when this enlarges our hearts to love the giver and declare His goodness to others, with a desire to honor and obey Him; and when we frame ourselves in all conditions to thankfulness— then it is a mighty and powerful means to soften the hard heart and hold under the heart's strong corruptions (such as impatience, discontentment, wrath, and anxiety in our afflictions), so that it might thereby become subject to God, even when there are strong provocations to the contrary.

We cannot then be ignorant that thankfulness is one help—and that not the least—to the continuation of a godly life, whether we understand it of that solemn thanksgiving which we ordinarily join to our supplications, or the brief thanksgiving which we occasionally offer.

So, we have looked at thanksgiving. To this we must add supplications or requests, which include the confession of our sins. These three parts are generally included in the one act of prayer, but each one has a special use. Therefore, we will now show how we should make confession of our sins and then our private requests to God, that together they may help us to godliness, although one part—namely, thanksgiving—is by itself such a great help.

The Second Part of Private Prayer: Confession of Sin

Now we turn to the confession of our sins, as it is the next in order to be used after thankfulness. After this, we will explain the offering up of our requests to God, especially for the remission of sins and other favors, with which it is ordinarily joined.

What Confession Is

Confession is an acknowledging of ourselves to be guilty (Ps. 32:5–6; 1 John 1:8–9) and deserving of God's wrath and His many punishments for our grievous faults and offenses. And it is an acknowledging of our sins with a free and humble bewailing of them before the Lord. For those sins which are unknown to us, we do this in a general manner; but for those which we do know (according to their nature), we confess specifically.

Four Things in Confession

We rightly practice the duty of confession when, first, we feel our sins odious and burdensome to us; secondly, when we accuse ourselves of our sins to God; thirdly, when having examined our life, we confess that we stand at His mercy, deserving to be condemned; fourthly, when we abase ourselves by confession, so that we are humbled and our pride is abated.

These four things are found in all the confessions of God's servants. I can show this at once without saying much about every one of them. Consider David's confession (2 Sam. 12:13) after the prophet Nathan accused him, saying, "Thou art the man"—that is, this great offender. He answered, "I have sinned." In this one word, he showed all the things that are required in a true and penitent confession. He showed his hatred of his sin; he accused himself to God; he confessed that he had justly provoked God against him; and he was greatly humbled by it. If any doubt this, he may see these things particularly described in Psalm 51 (cf. vv. 4–5).

The same may be said of Daniel's confession in Daniel 9 (cf. v. 5), and in the publican's. When beating on his breast and looking down to the ground as one ashamed to look up, he said, "God be merciful to me a sinner" (Luke 18:13).

These things are also in the confession of the prodigal son. First, in the words, "he came to himself" (15:17), we see how he considered his past life and felt his burden so great. Secondly, he came and accused himself to his father. Thirdly, when he asked not for mercy or to be counted as a son, we can see what he felt he deserved (v. 21). And fourthly, we see his abasement in that he thought it a large favor to have the place of a hired servant (vv. 19–21).

How Confession Is a Help to Godliness

By this we can see the manner of confession we should ordinarily use in our prayers to God. If we frame confession otherwise—that is, out of our own thoughts—God will reject it. Seeing this, we will not coldly confess our sins in a general way (as many do, with little comfort), nor for show, but specifically, and especially those by which we have most offended God (1 Sam. 12:20).

The frequent practice of confessing our sins to God will not suffer us to go far into any sin or stay in it for long. Rather, we will hunt it out before it is warm and nestled within our hearts. When in coming to confess our sins we see how they burden us, though they are not committed willfully but through negligence and infirmities, who does not see that by confessing them in this manner we will be preserved from dangerous falls and reproachful offenses? Therefore, the confession of our sins, which is but one aspect of prayer, is a powerful force to strengthen us in living a godly life.

An Objection Answered

To those who object that frequently performing this duty will make it too commonplace with no force to kill our sin, I answer thus: having promised by this and other similar helps to chain up the unruliness of our nature, God grants grace and liberty to His servants (despite the rebellion that remains in them) much to prevail against it, so that they may ordinarily find ease and peace by these helps. In so doing, they also find a cheerful readiness to use them (which puts away tediousness), much more than those who by custom in earthly matters find hard things easy.

The Third Part of Private Prayer: Request

Having shown how thanksgiving and confession of sin should be used and how using them are helps to godliness, it now remains to explain making requests to God, how requests should be made, and the fruit of godliness that may be reaped thereby.

Request is the part of prayer in which we earnestly pour out our supplications unto God in contrition of heart according to His will with a comforting hope that through Christ we will be heard; and therefore, forsaking the sin which might hinder our supplications, we wait patiently. There are thus five things necessary in making our requests.

Contrition of Heart

The first thing in request is that we show contrition of heart (1 Sam. 1:15) by being pressed with the feeling of our wants, unworthiness, miserable condition, and many necessities, while earnestly desiring to be pardoned and eased. This will not be found difficult if our confession of sins is sincere and according to the previously mentioned rules. For the one who most sincerely accuses himself (Luke 18:13) is the same who can most freely offer requests to God. Our praying to God is cold and counterfeit when we are not touched with our own vileness (Matt. 5:3); and thus we better feel our necessities, which we desire to have relieved (Ps. 145:19). But if this is so, we will neither pray in word only, which God abhors, nor think ourselves too good to wait upon God (if He does not at first grant our requests), but will continue in them (Matt. 15:28) as He commands (Luke 18:1).

Praying according to His Will
The second thing in request is that we ask God for nothing except that which He according to His Word allows us to pray for and are therefore agreeable to His will. We will not pray in vain, then, when we pray for those things which He has promised we will obtain. The apostle therefore says, "This is the confidence that we have in him, that, if we ask any thing according to his will, he heareth us" (1 John 5:14; cf. John 14:13; 15:7; 16:24). As this rule suffers us not to seek after our own will and desires, so it is no small benefit to us; for He gives whatever we stand in need of if we ask according to His will. And who would desire to have that which our loving, generous Father sees is not good for us? If this does not satisfy some, consider that they ask but they obtain not, because they "ask amiss" (James 4:3). Furthermore, though they think themselves good Christians, they lose all their labor in praying when they move their lips, while God meanwhile counts their supposed devotion as much babbling and curses it as being done in ignorance of His will.

Encouragement That We Will Be Heard through Christ
From this arises the third thing in request, that we should quicken ourselves to frequently and cheerfully

come in faith and confidence (James 1:6), seeing that God has given us such great encouragement and such precious promises of so many great things. We should go to God in the same way that people go to their trustworthy neighbors with good hope to borrow, when their neighbors have often before promised to lend.

It is no marvel that people seldom and reluctantly pray when they lack faith and the assurance of obtaining what they request. But God in His great wisdom and love bids us rejoice in bringing our prayers to Him by believing that we will receive. This is seen in that which He says in John's Gospel, "Ask, and ye shall receive, that your joy may be full" (16:24). He says this because there are many things throughout our lives to make us sad and heavy, and because in our natural disposition we are slow and unwilling to pray and distrustful when we offer our requests. If through lack of experience we are not fully resolved that we both should and may pray with cheerfulness and gladness, considering God our most loving Father who cannot forget His kindness toward us, then we should be persuaded of this from the fruits reaped by prayer. These effects of prayer will easily draw us to prayer with delight, though the flesh holds us backward as with cords—some of which effects I will briefly set down, and they are especially three.

The first effect is that by prayer we are made acquainted with God (James 4:8). Being admitted to speak to Him, we come to know His mind and will and how He is affected toward us (John 16:26; Rev. 3:20). The second effect of prayer is that it gives life to God's graces within us, such as faith, hope, and care of duty. These lay half dead within us until they are revived by bellows of prayer. For we are dull, forgetful, unprofitable, and faint in hope. Our comfort is often dim. Yet in and after prayer we are well refreshed again, even as the first is quickened by blowing. We see this in the worthy example of Queen Esther, who before prayers to God was fearful, as we may gather. Yet she was mightily encouraged and strengthened after prayer in a most powerful way unlikely to be obtained. The third effect of prayer is that in our greatest need it brings the good gifts of God which our souls desire. As it is written, "Ask, and it shall be given you" (Matt. 7:7). Indeed, prayer brings things we once could not expect, such as joy in heaviness, light in darkness, and hope for despair, as we see in the song of Hannah (1 Sam. 2:1–2), following her effectual prayer (1:10).

Forsaking Our Sins

But I will proceed to the fourth property of request in prayer, that when we pray, we bring not the sins which will turn away the Lord's ears from hearing us. These sins are any that we do not renounce and repent from, but rather secretly nourish in our hearts. Solomon confirms this when he says, "He that turneth away his ear from hearing the law, even his prayer shall be abomination" (Prov. 28:9). David agrees with him, saying as he poured out his requests to God, "If I have done this; if there be iniquity in my hands; if I have rewarded evil unto him that was at peace with me," or have plundered my enemy without cause (Ps. 7:3–4), will not God find it out? But when we make our requests to God with these properties (for in this manner God requires them to be offered), we will reap no small fruit. For the Christian who observes these things, whether he plead for remission of his sins or any good thing he needs, or against any calamity or burden with which he is distressed, by this he will surely prevail with God for others and for himself. What encouragement, do you think, this adds to a godly life?

Waiting Patiently

The last thing required in rightly making our requests is to wait patiently upon God for the outcome to see what end He will grant of our petitions. When this grace is missing, it takes away the grace of our supplications. Yet we are very prone to impatience, for we are content with nothing less than what we have prayed for. But we must bridle this weakness, for we do not know what the Lord will do, whether He will grant our desires or answer some other way. Therefore, the prophet who had good experience of God's fatherly providence toward His faithful servants exhorts them to wait upon Him when they have once commended their way unto Him, assuring them that whatever is best for them, that God will bring to pass (37:5). And this patience, which is such a near companion to faith, holds the mind in a sweet quietness, even before we see God's answer. Since this is so, who can deny that this makes our prayer well pleasing to God and therefore with the previously mentioned properties is a great help in performing our duties?

How Private Prayer Is a Help to Godliness

Having explained these properties for rightly making requests to God, consider how prayer is a help to godliness. For when these three parts of God's worship—namely, thanksgiving, confession, and request—are reverently and humbly joined together (for they usually belong together in our prayers [cf. James 4:8–10]), they have great force and power to uphold a godly life. For by confession of sins, a man acknowledges himself to be a guilty person and a debtor to God, and this makes him slower to continue in sin. By making his requests, he declares that he is a beggar, standing in need of all things and, if he knows himself well (Rev. 3:17), having nothing of his own except sin and filthiness. And by giving thanks he confesses that everything he has or enjoys he receives from God's mere mercy and bounty. Each of these parts to prayer helps him to see his infinite debt to God. They abate his pride, stir up his heart to seek God, and enlarge his heart to love and obey Him. If he is fallen, the prayer of faith raises him up; if he is heavy, prayer comforts him; and if he is dull, prayer quickens him. Who can count the infinite, marvelous commodities that come through prayer, when it is accompanied by these properties?

Therefore, seeing that prayer is a present remedy to the oppressed heart and a preserver of the godly mind and a giver of strength to the weak and a special means to make a man fit to live in every condition which God sets him, I conclude that it is a strong and mighty help to the godly life. If you pray well, you will live well. If you keep yourself fit to perform this duty as you have been directed, you do not need to fear any great annoyance in your life. But the way prayer along with some other helps is to be daily used, that the fruit of it may be more certain, will be set down in the next treatise on the daily direction, for that is a fitting place for it.[3]

---

3. See page 68, footnote 1 above.

CHAPTER 11

Reading

The next help to godliness is reading. This is an exercise and duty that the Christian (whom I seek to inform) may find helpful, together with the other means, in advancing a godly life. Therefore, I will provide some direction about this. And although much could be said about reading to benefit those who are more learned, yet I have applied myself throughout my whole book to help every Christian believer to walk on the way to heaven with more ease, fruit, and comfort. Therefore, I purpose to do the same here.

To this end, I will arrange what I must say in five questions and answers, thus including all my thoughts about this. First, what should be read? Second, who should read? Third, when should they read? Fourth, how should they read? And fifth, why should they read?

What Should Be Read?

The first question is, What should be read? The answer, first of all, is the Book of God, which is the book of books, even the canonical Scriptures of the Old and New Testaments. Then, secondly, other sound and godly books. For not all books that are in print should be read, not even if their content is good. For reading many books is wearisome to the flesh and can bring little profit or much hurt to the reader. This is to be avoided.

And of those which are to be read, some are most fit to inform the judgment and the understanding to make the reader wise and skillful in the knowledge of divine things. Some of these are John Calvin's *Institutes*, Peter Martyr Vermigli's *Common Places*, and Theodore Beza's *Confessions*.[1] Others help more specifically in practical knowledge by confirming faith and endeavoring to keep

---

1. Peter Martyr Vermigli (1499–1562) was an Italian Reformer. Many of his biblical commentaries were compiled together by a Huguenot preacher named Robert Masson and published in 1576 as *Loci Communes*, Latin for "Common Places." The French Reformer John Calvin (1509–1564) is famous for his work in Geneva, his legacy of expository preaching and biblical commentaries, and his *Institutes of the Christian Religion*, which has been translated into English several times. Theodore Beza (1519–1605) was Calvin's successor in Geneva. "*Confessions*" is Rogers's reference to Beza's *Confession De Foi Du Chretien*, published in Geneva in 1558 and translated into English by Robert Fills in c. 1562 as *A briefe and piththie summe of the Christian faith made in forme of a confession, with a confutation of all such superstitious errours, as are contrary therevnto.*

a good conscience. Of these which direct a Christian in living a godly life, this book in which I have travailed (I am not ashamed to say) is one tending to this end. Some books help in both doctrine and practice. Among these, the worthy labors of Master William Perkins are the principal of our time, containing in a clearer way the sum of many learned authors about the matter of Christianity.[2]

Seeing such books as have been mentioned should be read, it follows that men should therefore as their ability will permit have such books in their houses. Those who cannot purchase them should provide the best that may be obtained at a cheaper price by the help of their faithful and learned teachers—namely, sound and plain catechisms and godly sermons and treatises concerning faith and repentance. These should be viewed as another kind of household instrument, such as cards[3] and tables and other similar things, without which the house is thought to be naked. And further, when they have these books, they must be careful not to cast them into bench holes[4] nor suffer them to lie unoccupied and covered with cobwebs.

---

2. William Perkins (1558–1602), often called "the father of Puritanism," was an influential pastor, preacher, and theologian and one of Rogers's friends. Reformation Heritage Books is currently publishing a projected ten-volume edition of his *Works*.

3. A card is a toothed machine for carding wool.

4. A bench hole was the hole in a latrine. Rogers was evidently concerned that good books were being used as toilet paper!

For let the best know that if they do not use reading, they will find much more hindrance in their life—also unpleasantness, unquietness, unfruitfulness, and uncheerfulness, even though they use other helps. Furthermore, seeing that they should read books which are fit for building them up in godliness, they must not spend their time in reading filthy, lewd, and wanton books; nor books needless nor unprofitable; nor superstitious pamphlets; nor Niccolò Machiavelli's blasphemies[5] (for it is a shame these should be suffered to come into men's hands); nor the subtle devices and deceitful dreams and errors of the Church of Rome— except they be able for their sound judgment to discern them, so that they may be the better able to detest and give others warning of them.

Who Should Read?

The next question is, Who should read? The answer is, all people for whom good books are written. But they are written for all sorts, as St. John says in 1 John 2:12–14: I write unto you little "children," "young men," and "fathers." Therefore, all people ought to read. Seeing that the apostle writes to all, yet so few regard but rather dislike the reading of books, I will say more.

---

5. Niccolò Machiavelli (1469–1527) was an Italian humanist during the Renaissance period, whose books rationalized unscrupulous and immoral behavior among politicians. His most famous book is *The Prince* (1513).

Little Children

Many say there is little reason why children should be urged to read. But St. John in requiring this duty of them puts to shame those who count it needless and almost ridiculous to require this duty of children. For thus he says, "I write unto you, little children, because ye have known the Father" (1 John 2:13). By this he shows us that children who are in years a degree under young men are capable of a true and saving knowledge of God, and that among them in his time were those who knew God to be their Father through Christ their Mediator. And may not those who have been trained up by their godly parents to hear the same doctrine preached to them till they have either attained to the grace of believing or at least do see so much into the beauty of it that they do earnestly and unfeignedly desire and long after the same—may not these read good books with savor and sweetness? Such was Timothy, who was brought up in the Scriptures from his childhood, and the children of the elect lady in 2 John, for they walked in the truth. And if they could savor faith, they were also fit to be framed to a Christian life. Now then, if children are capable of these great and precious things, of knowing God and walking after His will, is it not shameful to say children should not be drawn to read? Does this not argue that the apostle was not well advised, when he wrote to children to the end that they might read? Therefore, though the profane and irreligious people who do not love reading are led with error, yet let the well-advised Christian know that children are to be exercised in reading good books.

Young Men

The second sort of people who should read good books are young men, who should fight against the devil and his instruments with their spiritual weapons and prevail against them by their holy courage and manhood. "I write unto you young men, because you have overcome the evil one," says the apostle. For they make the Word of God, which they hear and read (as it is called the sword of the Spirit), a principal help and means to vanquish Satan and overcome their unruly lusts, which wait for them in mischief and would, if it were possible, bring them to utter destruction. And they well prove this if, as unmarried, they care for the things of the Lord. And if not, that they are subject to the apostle's precept to Titus, that they be sober—that is, well-governed. For so he says there in one word: "Young men likewise exhort to be sober minded" (Titus 2:6). Now therefore, seeing young men have so many strong enemies to fight against, as all their corruptions are, and those (as it were) set on fire by hell, there is good reason that they along with others should be diligent in searching the Scriptures and in daily reading of other good books. They should read to establish and strengthen themselves against their enemies and corruptions and to edify and build themselves up in their most holy faith. In this way they prove that young men of God's nurturing will prosper and thrive far better than such as walk after their own heart's desire, scorning good books and the reading of them.

Fathers

And as for old men to whom he writes, unless they are a reproach to their gray hairs, they know the great works of God, having not only read them in the history of God's Word, but also having marked them and observed them in their own experience. They have seen how God has threatened and pursued His enemies, the disobedient, and how He has been good and gracious to His beloved servants. Therefore, they should be easily persuaded to read, having such good encouragement from times past. Those who take no pleasure in this, but with the common sort of older people delight to hear and tell tales and to laugh and be merry in a vain and profane manner, they are not those to whom the apostle wrote. They are those who should rather be bewailed as being unsavory to others. And they should be ashamed of themselves, if they are not utterly blind and brutish. But the old men to whom the apostle wrote were fathers—as he says, "I write unto you fathers," that they might be examples in gravity, integrity, wisdom, and in other good things, and therefore might continue their course in reading, besides their use of means, to bring their gray hairs with peace unto their graves. And these should give themselves to reading and not (as most do) to foolish talking, idleness, and worldliness.

When Should They Read?

The third question is, When should they read? This question cannot be as quickly or easily answered as the former. Ministers are expressly commanded to attend to reading—that is, to give themselves to it daily with all diligence as part of their particular calling (unless some special occasion do hinder at some time), and that also of more necessity at this time. But other men have their several callings to follow. And we must not lay burdens upon them which God has not laid and therefore are too heavy for them to bear by requiring of them duties which they cannot perform—neither therefore this duty of reading. But this must be wisely received, for we are not to nourish in sloth those who are too reluctant to read, of which sort there are too many. For do we think that the Holy Ghost exempts any from it? Why then does He move all to read (as we have seen) and pronounce them blessed who join reading together with the practice of what they read (Rev. 1:3)?

What then is to be done, seeing none are exempt from reading, neither are any bound to it in the same way as the minister? I answer, as a man has more freedom and liberty in his calling than another and fewer hindrances and more encouragements and help by wealth and ability, so the more time he should give to reading. And those who come behind in these things must be content with less use and exercise in reading. And they may rest with peace, although they cannot enjoy the benefit so freely and fully as some others. For as some who receive the Word into a good and honest heart bring forth thirty-fold, some sixty-fold, and some a hundred-fold, even so, some cannot use as many means nor use them so often as some others, and thus do not attend so much to reading. But let all who look for fruit keep and show an honest and good conscience in doing what they can. Let them earnestly stir themselves up to this, knowing how much reluctance there is in our flesh, such as dullness, coldness, unwillingness, yea and rebellion against it. For if men give place to the flesh, they will hardly begin and only go forward with more difficulty. And if they are unfit to read one good thing, then let them read another (for in reading, men are like sick people with food—they have irritable stomachs). Set often before them the benefit of reading and how many ways they may benefit from it, as will be explained after this. And let them again consider why they suspend their practice of reading at any time, and whether it is for weightier occasions and not rather to seek liberty to the flesh and to rove after their own fantasies. Some who cannot observe any ordinary practice in reading must read when they can. But others who have more leisure and liberty for reading should be careful to keep their practice constant, especially when they first begin. And when they break it off because of necessity, let them make it up at some other time. And let them not read for show (as some used to do), but let them sincerely desire to benefit from it. Moreover, they should not read superstitiously, putting holiness in the deed done, as if the act of reading itself—whatever their intentions may be—pleases God.

But regardless of the rules given about reading, I cannot sufficiently bewail the condition of those who seldom read, only when they must, or for fear or shame, or for curious novelty. These faults are too commonly committed even by Christians. For some of them, since they follow the world in one way or another, can find no leisure in reading. Others, taking their full scope in play and pleasures, cannot attend to such sad matters (as they count them), though they welcome the others. Others neglect the good work of this necessary duty through idleness and sloth, or with swarms of vain thoughts or dangerous lusts carrying them, or through gross ignorance, or needless and idle talk. But if they had learned to make conscience of it, they might shake off much annoyances by watching their opportunities, by which they would have no need to fear that their labor in reading would be plentifully rewarded. As for binding anyone to read something daily, though it is a good help to those who can and do, yet it should not be imposed upon anyone by necessity; nor does God require this. But as any can give time to it, he may be certain that he will lose nothing thereby, but will benefit greatly.

How Should They Read?

In the fourth place, it is asked how they should read and by what means they should be directed in it. This is important to learn and observe. For we should not think that everyone who picks up a book to read when he is disposed or who occasionally reads for novelty should expect to profit by his reading. But as reading gives great hope of benefit if it is well regarded, so people must take good heed in how they use it. And although for those who are learned and for students of theology the understanding of arts and languages and the knowledge of the Scripture's manners of expression and similar things are great helps, to which private persons cannot attain, yet there are many helps for them also by which they can attain that knowledge which is most suited to guide, quicken, and comfort them while they live here.

The first requirement is that he who desires to make good use of his reading should be soundly catechized and well instructed in the principles of Christian religion. In this way, being made a sound Christian by the assurance of his salvation and his sanctification he may grow in it by reading as he does by other helps. Otherwise, though he has both wit and will to read and hear many other good things, yet he will never have the right use of them. He will rather be like those who have many household instruments to use but no house in which to place them. So, he may have many fragments of knowledge and skill which are able to do some good to others, but he will be without the chief good himself because he lacks that for which all these things should serve as helps. Not only is the common hearer none the better, although he sometimes reads, but even he who is occasionally moved to joy and sorrow by his hearing and reading yet is not helped to heaven or holiness, because his heart is not well seasoned with saving knowledge, which is the beginning of anything that is good. For as his good motions and affections quickly rise, so they quickly fall and vanish as sparks of the furnace in the air. But if he is thus grounded, in his reading he must understand what he reads in order to hold it in agreement with the fundamental points of the catechism. This will be a means to keep him from many errors. It will also be a good help for him to clearly understand the sum and contents of the various chapters he reads with the drift and scope of the whole book, as well as the things that go before and follow any difficult place. He will also be more enlightened and helped in reading if he digests his reading by meditating on it afterward. To all this, he who can add the reading of sound interpreters, taking the opportunity to confer with the learned, will find much fruit and profit by his reading.

Why Should We Read?

Now follows the fifth and final question: Why should we read? In general, the answer is so that we will know and practice what we read. Yet seeing that the Scripture more specifically sets down the purposes of reading, it will be clearer to us if we consider them. Now the purposes for which Scripture is written are the purposes for which we should use them, both in our reading and hearing. There are five purposes, four of which are mentioned in St. Paul's second epistle to Timothy, where he says, "All scripture is given by inspiration of God, and is profitable for doctrine, for reproof, for correction, for instruction in righteousness" (3:16). The fifth purpose in reading, as seen in Romans 15:4, is that we may be comforted.

Doctrine

The first purpose—namely, to teach or instruct us—is worthily set in the first place, for all the others depend upon it. For until we know the truth and understand the will of God (each person in his measure), we can neither condemn anything as error neither find any fault in our life nor amend it nor be comforted by it. Knowledge, therefore, is the first to enlighten us, and by it we have use of the rest. We should read that we may get understanding in all the parts of the will of God—such as to know God rightly, how He is to be rightly served and believed in, and how we should walk through this our pilgrimage and afterward attain and enjoy the presence of God and joy thereby forever. Without this, what a dark and dead life this is! If this were duly considered, men would be constrained to confess it. For they walk in darkness. And who does not know how uncomfortable it is to walk in darkness? Were it not that men deceive themselves with the persuasion that their best happiness is found in following the devices and desires of their own hearts, they would not be able to live out a tenth of their lives without weariness, deadly anxiety, and even madness itself. For all their self-deception, many come to no better condition, especially if they know that this understanding I speak of can be had and enjoyed, yet they themselves do not have it. For to be without an effectual and saving knowledge is both brutish and miserable, as Solomon declares somewhat covertly when he says that without knowledge the heart is "not good" (Prov. 19:2). Thus, he condemns all who though they have some literal knowledge yet live shamefully and offensively, as they must, since their hearts are filthy and evil.

Reproof

The second purpose of reading is the refuting of errors and false doctrine, such as popery, Judaism, Islam, and the rest. And although it is primarily required of ministers to cut them off by the sword of the Spirit, as it is his primary duty to teach, correct, and comfort, yet it also pertains to all private Christians (as they can attain it) to discern false doctrine by the true measuring rod of God's Word—and in so doing to take heed that they be not perverted and spoiled by false doctrine, but abhor it and flee from it, as from a serpent. Those who through catechizing and by living under a sound, profitable ministry are well grounded in the knowledge of the principles will by their reading be able to discern and avoid many dangerous errors. St. John therefore commands the Christians to whom he wrote as well as their teachers to try the spirits (1 John 4:1), which breathed out doctrine among them, whether they were of God or no. And our Savior commands us to "beware of false prophets" (Matt. 7:15). And in Acts 17:11, the men of Berea and Thessalonica are commended for trying the apostle's doctrine by the Scriptures. This shows that they could do this, although they had only known the Scriptures for a short while. This was no small benefit to them, as others will also find when having attained sound and saving knowledge of the truth they are able to single out errors, as the Bereans did, in their readings.

Correction

The third purpose of reading is that all vices, sins, and faults that they read about in the Scriptures or any other sound author, they condemn them for their own parts as odious things which God cannot abide—and therefore, especially in themselves, if they see any such lie lurking either secretly within them or cleaving to them in their behavior and outward actions. And they should apply to themselves all such reproofs of sins as they will meet within their readings as forbidden to them and condemned in them. And if anyone of that sort hereafter joins with them and deceives them, they should censure them in like manner.

Training in Righteousness

The fourth purpose of reading is that whatsoever duties or gracious actions they read to be commanded of God, those they take to be commanded to themselves to show forth in their lives and to give good example thereby. The Lord has thus appointed their reading to be with other good helps the means to flee evil and do good, and (in a word) to live well. Both these things are effected by Him. And those who are made such have honest and good hearts, into the which they receive the Word and good instruction. And this is a singular end of reading, to advance this reformation in God's people.

Comfort

The fifth and last purpose of reading is to gain comfort by the four former purposes. For those who reap that fruit by their reading which they do by their hearing— to know the way to happiness, to discern the byways, and to follow their knowledge in practicing that which is good and declining the evil—may for good cause be comforted. Yes, that comfort will abide. And without this there is no other sound comfort that will stand by a man in his greatest need. And (to say no more of this) if the purpose of the Scriptures and thus the result of reading them be to comfort us, how are they deceived, even grossly bewitched, who think that no sound comfort can come from this, but think rather that reading (if they should exercise themselves in it) would take all delight and comfort from them?

A Few Observations about Reading

Therefore, to say no more of these five purposes of reading than necessary, I will conclude with a few observations and watchwords.

The first thing to be observed is that in reading the Scriptures they should not read a chapter here and there (except upon some good occasion), but rather read the Bible in order throughout and as often as they can. In this way (having already been established in the grounds of the Christian religion), they gradually become acquainted with the histories and the whole course of the Scriptures and so may gain a more comforting and generous use of them.

Furthermore, that which I have said about laying the grounds of Christian religion is well to be marked; for when these are by apt and fit coherences laid together in the mind and work upon the heart of the believing Christian, they are able to make the reading of other good books (and especially the Book of books, which is the Book of God) clear in many respects and profitable.

But it will seem to others who lack this as a closed book or full of obscurity and hard difficulties.

In reading other good books, I counsel them to read one or two well-written books, either about the whole Christian religion or any particular argument, and to read them often. Let them do this instead of reading a page here and a chapter there, as idle readers do for the sake of novelty. I say this because most Christians see too little into a good book in reading it just once or twice. Much less is the use of its doctrine reaped and enjoyed by dull heads, slippery memories, and those weak in practice. Since most people do not have the leisure to read many books, they will find the most profit by diligently going over the same books often and by choosing the best and most necessary books by the help of their faithful teachers.

The Manner of Reading

Now concerning the manner of reading, in addition to what I have said before, it must be with: (1) a sincere intention to learn and profit by it, desiring God to prepare us with reverence and to enlighten our understandings that we may conceive that which we read; and (2) settling ourselves for the time of our reading to be attentive and to abandon the wandering of the heart, as much as may be. This will be more easily done in reading if it is well watched over (as has been said before) in our course of living.

Likewise, to make use of the Scriptures as the apostle requires when he says that all Scripture is given by inspiration of God, and is profitable to teach, convince, to correct, and instruct in righteousness, we must apply to ourselves all the general promises made to the faithful in the Scriptures and let all the exhortations and admonitions quicken and stir us up from coldness, deadness, and drowsiness. We must let all reprehensions check us for faults escaped, and all threats frighten our boldness and appall our presumption, which is too easily and readily kindled in us. And we must make use of the Scriptures in matters not only concerning God but also those concerning men, and men of all kinds—whether prince and subject, noble and base, men and women, and more particularly in families: husbands and wives, parents and children, masters and servants. To read, therefore, that we may by reading be made fit unto every good work and thus glorify God thereby is undoubtedly to make our reading a special help and means to grow and advance in a godly life, as it is appointed of God.

But this one thing I cannot omit: that seeing the benefit and comfort of this exercise of reading is so great; and that the substance of the Scriptures is now brought to light as it is, both in our own language and in the interpretation of them (both of which popery has a long time deprived us of); and that such variety of good books have been granted to us by God—that yet even those who look for eternal life delight so little in them. For I speak not of the profane and unruly, whom nothing will move to read nor even to hear sermons, till God causes them to see how they have deceived themselves. But I am sure it is one special cause why so many learned and godly men are discouraged from putting any new works in print, for they see the professors of the gospel bestow so little labor and time in reading those which are already available.

I think it will be helpful to add two things in regard to some Christians who have not the gift of reading. First, that they endeavor to follow the above rules by using the help of others, exhorting all by their loss and disadvantage to more highly esteem reading. And secondly, that in addition to the former rules those who have better helps of understanding, memory, and leisure should note their doubts and as they have opportunity seek resolution of them at their learned pastor's hands.

How Reading Is a Help to Godliness

And though there are other things besides these which the more learned may take profit by, as I have said, yet since they are more out of the reach for the greatest number of Christians, they do not so nearly nor necessarily concern them. And it must be remembered that I did not intend to say everything that could be said about reading, but only to show how it may be profitably used to help the Christian be fruitful in a godly life.

For whoever considers how many ways the conscience is appeased, the judgment enlightened and enlarged, the heart persuaded, the memory relieved, the affections moved, and, in a word, the whole man drawn by that which he reads—they will have no doubt how great, together with the other helps, the benefit of reading is to the teachable Christian. By using it as often as possible in the manner I have prescribed, with so many things received by us in our reading, who could doubt that it will be a singular help and furtherance to a godly Christian life? For a mind that was well seasoned before will undoubtable be better seasoned and refreshed when it often by reading drinks the water of life from the sweet fountain of God's Word.

CHAPTER 12

Solemn Thanksgiving and Fasting

Finally, we will consider the extraordinary helps which are not used daily, but occasionally, according to the extraordinary times the Lord offers. There are two extraordinary helps: solemn thanksgiving and fasting, joined with extraordinary prayer.

Solemn Thanksgiving

The first extraordinary help is solemn thanksgiving. This is when by God's command and the examples of the godly who have gone before us in a most fervent way we yield praise to God, rejoicing in sincere remembrance and consideration of some unusual deliverance from desperate danger. In solemn thanksgiving, we also bind ourselves more firmly to the Lord in renewing our holy covenant, testifying this by signs of sincere good will to our brethren.

This is seen most clearly in the famous example of Esther and Mordecai (for the sake of brevity, I mention no other), who with the rest of God's people were appointed by Haman's subtlety and cruel malice to be slain. Yet by prayer and fasting they obtained deliverance, when to man's judgment all hope was past (Est. 4:16; 9:1). They obtained not only deliverance but also their hearts' desire against their adversaries, great favor of the king (a strong enemy whom God made into a mighty friend), and much wealth and prosperity. For this reason, they appointed a day and time in the which the Lord might be praised, that they might express their joy and send "portions one to another" to testify their love unto them (vv. 18, 22).

This is that solemn thanksgiving which I call one of the extraordinary helps to advance us in godliness, which is to be offered up to God by all His people in similar occasions. Such occasions are distinct from daily thanksgiving in their fervency of spirit and the length of time devoted to it. When it is publicly performed as belonging to the whole church, as occasion requires, this duty should be accompanied with the preaching of the word. For this quickens the assembly to the more earnest profession of their thankfulness, just as the solemn feasts under the law were performed with a holy convocation. If the cause for this extraordinary help is private and concerns one person alone (or a family or just a few people), then it should be privately offered by them with psalms, praise of His name, and declaration of His works, with the reading of Scriptures (such as Psalms 105–7) for this purpose.

One place in Scripture very suited to this purpose, which teaches a most helpful way of practicing this duty whether publicly or privately, is that appointed by David, the man of God, in setting up the ark of God in the tabernacle. Some of the words are these: "Give thanks unto the LORD, call upon his name, make known his deeds among the people. Sing unto him, sing psalms unto him, talk ye of all his wondrous works. Glory ye in his holy name: let the heart of them rejoice that seek the LORD" (1 Chron. 16:8–10; cf. vv. 11–19; 19:10–15).

Fasting

The other extraordinary help is fasting, joined with most fervent prayer. Fasting is a most earnest profession of deep humbling of ourselves in abstinence, with confession of sins and supplications (for at least the greatest part of the day) to God, to turn away some sore calamity from us or for obtaining of some special blessing. I will briefly expound upon this description for those who perhaps have not read or heard much about the exercise of fasting and have no books at hand to help them use it rightly.

Humility

In fasting, we must be deeply humbled and make earnest profession of it, more than in the ordinary abasing of ourselves. For though we ought to do this sincerely and deeply as often as we pray and confess our sins, yet we cannot do so with the same measure of fervency or for the same length of time as we should in this exercise.

Abstinence

With this profession of our humiliation, we must join abstinence. By this I mean that we must deprive ourselves of the lawful pleasures and liberties of this life, such as food and drink (more than for necessity), costly apparel, and earthly matters (which we are otherwise free to enjoy), thus declaring that we by our sins have made ourselves unworthy of them.

Duration

It must also be done for the most part of the day—that is, to the end that by this long time of humiliation and abasement our hearts may be more cast down and thoroughly touched with our distressed estate, than they are likely to be in a shorter time.

Supplications

Supplications, containing our requests and our confession of sins, are added to teach us that the chief part of this exercise consists in prayer.

When Fasting Should Be Used

It is understood that this is done for the removing of some great calamity (2 Chron. 20:6), either of some painful affliction outwardly hanging over us or the whole church (or already upon us) or some grievous sin that we have committed or have long continued in. For when weaker means do not remove such sins and afflictions from us, these extraordinary means are enjoined by the Lord to deliver us from them, wholly or in part, or else to content us (Dan. 3:18) that we may rest ourselves in God that His grace will be sufficient for us (2 Cor. 12:9).

As with thanksgiving, so with fasting: when done publicly, we require the benefit of sermons and fit Scriptures to stir us up; when done in private, we must meditate on similar Scriptures for the well carrying of ourselves through such a weighty business. But in both, let this be regarded: that we take them not in hand except we come in true and unfeigned repentance. As surely as we come in this way, so sure may we be that God will be present with us and hear us. And this will make the whole action more pleasant and the outcome more comforting. For as we began our fast mournfully, as we had good cause, the Lord having humbled us and sending us to testify our sincere grief by such abasement, so having sought and pled to His majesty with sincere repentance we may lift up ourselves again and be comforted in heart. For He has promised to most graciously accept such a sacrifice (Joel 2:13; Hos. 14:2–3).

How Solemn Thanksgiving and Fasting Are Helps to Godliness

Having therefore explained the nature and quality of these extraordinary helps, who can deny that they both are most effectual means to advance us in the godly life? This is clear if we duly consider the force and use of each one in their proper times. For thanksgiving raises us up to a joyful remembrance of God's wonderful kindness, while fasting brings us low as we remember our vileness. Both greatly draw our hearts in more love and obedience to God. We thus see how they are helps to godliness.

CONCLUSION

Several Cautions for Rightly Using the Helps

To conclude this whole treatise on the helps, I wish to give you a few cautions, diligent reader, to the end that you may have the right use of them.

Understand the helps well. The first caution is for you to thoroughly consider and understand well the helps and the benefits which they may bring, and so with a quiet and meek heart set upon them in the manner that has been explained. And encourage yourself to this, for seeing that some have such great power for well framing the heart and life (each in its own way), how much more will using all of them together bring a large and generous blessing in this way?

Esteem the helps highly. As they are precious and have an excellent purpose, so you should hold still the greatest account and estimation of them, and use them with the greatest reverence, as your frailty will permit.

Do not use the helps for show. Do not use the helps for fashion or show, as the counsel of the flesh will be, for in a short time this makes the best things vile.

Use the helps constantly. Give no place to weariness and slackness in using them, either when you first begin or after long continuance.

Confess your failures. Be diligent and ready to search out your faults, if they come upon you unexpectedly or any other way. Do not hide them, but check your corrupt heart and confess them to the Lord in secret, and He will hear and forgive you. Then set upon the use of these helps again in a fresh way, even as you did before.

Helps for Meditation

Let us search and try our ways, and turn again to the LORD.

—Lamentations 3:40

1. Let us keep a narrow watch over our hearts, words, and deeds continually (Ps. 39:1; Eph. 5:15; 1 Peter 1:15).

2. Let us with all care redeem the time, which has been idly, carelessly, and unprofitably spent (Eph. 5:16; Col. 4:5).

3. Let us use private prayer and meditation at least once a day (Col. 4:2).

4. Let us take care to both do and receive good when in company with others (Luke 14:15–16; Heb. 10:24).

5. Let us instruct, watch over, and govern our families with diligence (Gen. 18:19; Deut. 4:9; 6:7; Prov. 31:27).

6. Let us bestow no more time or care than necessary to matters of the world (Col. 3:2).

7. Let us stir ourselves up to generosity to God's saints (Gal. 6:10; Heb. 13:16).

8. Let us not give the least bridle to wandering lusts and affections (Eph. 5:3–4; Col. 3:5).

9. Let us prepare ourselves to bear the cross, in whatever means it pleases God to exercise us (Matt. 16:24).

10. Let us give some time in mourning not only for our own sins but also for the sins of the time and age in which we live (Lam. 1:1; Dan. 9:3–20).

11. Let us look daily for the coming of our Lord Jesus Christ for our full deliverance out of this life (1 Cor. 1:7; Titus 2:13).

12. Let us (as we have opportunity, or at least as we have necessity) acquaint ourselves with some godly and faithful person with whom we may discuss our Christian condition and open our doubts for the quickening up of God's graces in us (James 5:16).

13. Let us observe the departure of men out of this life—their mortality, the vanity and mutability of things below—that we may lightly esteem the world and continue our longing after the life to come. And let us meditate and muse often upon our own death and departure from this life, and how we must lie in the grave and put off all our glory; for this will serve to beat down the pride of life that is in us (Eccl. 7:4; Phil. 1:23; Rev. 22:20).

14. Let us daily read something from the Holy Scriptures for the further increase of our knowledge (Deut. 17:19–20; Josh. 1:8; Ps. 1:2; Dan. 9:2).

15. Let us enter into covenant with the Lord to strive against all sin, and especially against the special sins and corruptions of our hearts and lives in which we have most dishonored the Lord and brought the most guilt upon our own consciences; and let us carefully keep and continue our covenant with God (2 Chron. 34:31; Neh. 9:38).

16. Let us mark how sin dies and is weakened in us, and let us wisely avoid all occasions to sin, that we turn not to our old sins

again (1 Thess. 5:22; 1 Peter 1:14; 2 Peter 2:20–22).

17. Let us fall not from our first love, but continue in our affections to delight in God's Word and all the holy exercises of religion, diligently hearing and faithfully practicing it in our lives and conversations. Let us prepare ourselves before we come and meditate and discuss that which we hear, either by ourselves or with others, and so mark our daily profiting in religion (Luke 8:13, 18; Rom. 2:13; James 1:19, 22; Rev. 2:4).

18. Let us often be occupied in meditating on God's benefits and works, and let us sound forth His praises for the same (Ps. 116:12–13; 118:15; Eph. 5:20).

19. Let us exercise our faith by taking comfort and delight in the great benefit of our redemption through Christ and the fulfillment of God's presence in His glorious and blessed kingdom (Phil. 1:23; 2 Tim. 4:7–8).

20. Lastly, let us not make these holy meditations and other similar practices of repentance a mere formality, neither let us use them for show.